UpperDogs

Christians Have The Advantage.
It's Time To Take It

SARAH THIESSEN
&
HEATHER HUGHES

WESTBOW
P R E S S®
A DIVISION OF THOMAS NELSON
& ZONDERVAN

Scriptures taken from the Holy Bible, New International Version®, NIV®. Copyright © 1973, 1978, 1984, 2011 by Biblica, Inc.™ Used by permission of Zondervan. All rights reserved worldwide. www.zondervan.com The "NIV" and "New International Version" are trademarks registered in the United States Patent and Trademark Office by Biblica, Inc.™ All rights reserved.

Interior Graphics/Art Credit: Isaac Hughes.

WestBow Press books may be ordered through booksellers or by contacting:

WestBow Press
A Division of Thomas Nelson & Zondervan
1663 Liberty Drive
Bloomington, IN 47403
www.westbowpress.com
844-714-3454

Because of the dynamic nature of the Internet, any web addresses or links contained in this book may have changed since publication and may no longer be valid. The views expressed in this work are solely those of the author and do not necessarily reflect the views of the publisher, and the publisher hereby disclaims any responsibility for them.

Any people depicted in stock imagery provided by Thinkstock are models, and such images are being used for illustrative purposes only. Certain stock imagery © Thinkstock.

ISBN: 978-1-4908-7443-2 (sc)
ISBN: 978-1-4908-7445-6 (hc)
ISBN: 978-1-4908-7444-9 (e)

Library of Congress Control Number: 2015904643

Print information available on the last page.

WestBow Press rev. date: 07/17/2015

Acknowledgements

To our Creator, there are not enough words. Thank you for, well, everything.

To our wonderful husbands, your devotion and endless support of our work is invaluable. Thank you both for being amazing men of God.

To our 7 collective children, thank you for your patience during writing days, for the valuable lessons you teach us and for being our biggest fans.

To our Splankna teammates, we couldn't do this without you. What you bring to the institute is priceless & treasured.

To our Family in Christ, you're beautiful and we love you.

To our many practitioners, your questions and eagerness for more keeps us on our toes. Your work in the world is beyond measure.

Contents

Church Of The Underdog..ix

Section 1 – Cultural Underdogs.. 1
    1. Cultural Passivity 3
    2. Cultural Aggression 11
    3. Downward Dog...17

Section 2 – UpperDog Ambassadors 29
    4. Love Wins...31
    5. Christians Have The Advantage 35
    6. Ambassadors in Action 78

Section 3 – Theological Underdogs.. 83
    7. Theological Passivity 85
    8. Theological Aggression 102
    9. Downward Dogs (again) 117

Section 4 – UpperDog Partners.. 121
    10. The Extremes...123
    11. Partnering in Authority...126
    12. Partnering In Creativity 139
    13. Partnering In Obedience...150
    14. Partnering In Prayer...182
           Variables...183
           The Faith Of Giants...184

Schrödinger's Dog 189
Drops In A Bucket.. 198
What Is Happening When We Pray........................... 199
Donation Matching 201
Imagination and Prayer 206
It's a Set-Up... 212
There's More To Your Part 215
An Honest Thank You.. 222
Creative Prayer... 223
15. Partner Splankna Style 228
16. Engage.. 237

Afterward – Partnership In Writing This Book 243
About The Authors..249
Endnotes..251

Church Of The Underdog

You might remember it. On October 3rd, 1964, NBC aired the first episode of their new animated series "Underdog." America loved it. He was a kindhearted, humble pup who would duck into a nearby telephone booth whenever his damsel was in distress and emerge a bumbling hero. Underdog tangled with several different nefarious characters in his day, typically causing considerable collateral damage in the process. But each show ended with the same scene: a crowd of people gazing upward with someone saying, "Look in the sky!" "It's a plane!" "It's a bird!" After this, an old woman wearing glasses would exclaim, "It's a frog!" Another onlooker would respond, "A frog?!?" To this, Underdog would reply with these words:

> *"Not plane, nor bird, nor even frog, it's just little old me...*
> (at this point, Underdog would usually crash into
> something, and then sheepishly finish...)
> *Underdog."*[1]

But we love him. Why? Because we can tell that he represents something true, something archetypal, something that relates to us. You see, underdog is a paradox. He is not what he seems. Imagine what it would be like if Underdog actually was the underdog. What would the show be like if he always lost? Would anyone be interested in watching? Of course not. He's intriguing because in spite of how he appears, and the name he's given, he's actually the champion. The contradiction is intriguing because it speaks of our own role in the story. Christians appear to be the underdogs as well, but it's an illusion.

We're actually the champions in the story. We're on the winning team and we're in the middle of that moment in the story where the winning team charges ahead—taking the lead to the roar of the crowd. This is the conquering scene and we have a big part in the action.

But we, the church of the 21ˢᵗ century, tend to live like we're in that part of the story where all the odds are stacked against us, like we're hunkered down in the midst of the enemy's camp just trying to survive. We live as if that's our only state until our Hero returns. Jesus, of course, is the Hero in this story. At least we've gotten that part right. He is the one who entered into human history, into this incredible tale and made the decisive move. This story ends with happily-ever-after because of him. But somehow we've missed a critical piece of information. We've overlooked the fact that while Jesus is the Hero,

We are his sidekicks.

We're not really underdogs. We're more like Robin to Batman or Tonto to the Lone Ranger. We have a critical role to play in this story. Where would the Hero be without his sidekick? Has God, in his insatiable quest for intimacy with us, made for himself children? Yes. Worshippers? Yes. Bride? Yes.

And Partners.

As his partners, as participants on the winning side, we are actually the UpperDogs in this story, no matter how things may feel at times. Think of this: after Jesus had accomplished the decisive move of the universe, his death and resurrection, he did not say, "Alright everyone, it's done. The story is finished. I came, I saw, I conquered. Let's celebrate!" He did not say this because while the decisive move had been made, the "battle won," the story was not over yet. Have you ever noticed that? Wouldn't you think the story would've been over at that moment? I mean, wasn't Jesus' grand entrance, epic battle and final surprising victory the whole point? We may not even realize it, but we live in this world as if the story has already climaxed and now it's just on pause. It's as if the important stuff is done and now we are just hanging out until the next big act begins in a land far, far away.

Are you familiar with recording artist David Wilcox? He's a world-class guitarist and song writer. His lyrics are incomparable. In one of his songs he talks about how Jesus' own life story culminated at age 33, and how that seems similar to the early deaths of so many celebrity greats… like Marilyn Monroe and James Dean. He playfully reasons that, "If you don't die in glory by the age of Christ, your story is just getting old."[2] Haven't you ever felt that way about the Christian story? Like it's just getting old? Without a clear sense of our purpose as partners, it's just a long, rather boring waiting game until the "sweet by and by."

If the average Christian asked himself, "Why is the story still going? What is this part for? What is my role in it?" I imagine that the gnawing, guilty responsibility to "evangelize" would surface as the most obvious answer, and rightfully so. We all know that Jesus' great last charge to his followers was to "go and make disciples of all the world."[3] But I contend that we've had too narrow a view of what that charge would look like. I believe that Jesus had much more in mind than our memorization of the "steps to salvation" and their occasional, awkward regurgitation. I believe he meant that his accomplishment through the empty tomb was now to be disseminated by us, to be manifested. And the manifestation of the Kingdom of God touches every arena of life. It isn't relegated to meetings at Panera Bread to explain Romans 3 (not that we shouldn't be doing quite a bit more of that).

Being disseminators of the Kingdom, representatives of the Truth and ambassadors of that which "draws all men unto him"[4] requires a *posture—a* new paradigm. It requires that we wrap our whole minds and hearts around how the reality of the gospel informs every facet of our demeanor—in culture, relationships, science and development, finance and faith. It is no longer sufficient (and maybe never was) for Christians to be differentiated by their purity alone. In order to fulfill our role in the story we're going to have to be known for more than what we avoid and disagree with.

Don't Drink, Don't Chew And Don't Go With Boys Who Do

My mother got an earful of that old adage growing up. Unfortunately though, that is predominantly what Christians are known for. What differentiates a Christian in the eyes of most non-believers is our long list of "don'ts." We're seen as the great sociological buzz-kill. We don't drink, we don't have sex, we don't know how to party. We're seen as judgmental and superior and foolish for it, like we don't realize how un-cool we really are. It reminds me of the Christian character in the Simpsons. Remember him? (Oh, come on, you watched it.) Ned Flanders was ever-nerdy, sickeningly sweet, super-conservative, passive and well, embarrassing—a definite, quintessential underdog. Rather than being esteemed or sought after, Christians are often seen as fringe, irrelevant outsiders. But the real problem here is not with the world and their opinion, it's with us. The problem is that largely we see *ourselves* this way.

We act as if we're prey in the wolves' territory, trembling and trying to stay safe until our great redeemer swoops in to make everything okay again. We think our highest goal is to keep ourselves from getting sullied in the world's big mud puddle—like we have to stay sheltered from them... protect our beliefs and hold on tight to each other in the great Red Rover game of life. We live like they have all the cards and we're bluffing.

But that is a lie.

We are the *UpperDogs.*

In every moment, every situation, every relationship, every idea or possibility, we have the upper hand. We are the ones who know the truth. We are the ones for whom death has lost its sting, rendering all threats empty. We are the ones with the ear of him who holds all resource, all potential, all power and authority, who has seen the story to its end and called it "good." We literally have all that every human being needs. We cannot be deceived, stolen from, humiliated or killed. We are the UpperDogs.

What if we knew it? What would it look like if we lived that way? What would it look like in our churches, in science, in politics, in relationships? How would it change the way we navigate a day, a prayer, a conversation? What if we realized that the upper hand is ours in every arena? What if we donned our sidekick capes and turned into meaningful players, respected contributors, co-movers in the story? How would it change the landscape of faith? What if we threw off the defensive posture and became UpperDogs?

The truth is that we are living in the *Partnership* act of the story. This is the scene in the big narrative where the hero and his sidekicks save the day. No matter how things may appear, Jesus is *still* the conqueror and this is *still* the conquering scene.

This is still the conquering scene.

We have a role to play and the advantage is ours. It's time we took it.

The Gist Of This Book

This book is intended for every Christian. It was written for the believer who longs for more, longs for faith to move beyond proposition into action. This book is for you. Of course there are many books on theology these days. Why did we feel the need to write another one? Two reasons. One is that our vantage point on the modern day body of Christ, from 10 years of training Christians around the country, has shown us the great need for this message—the message of advantage. The believers we regularly encounter struggle increasingly with the growing gap between the cultural and biblical norm. They struggle, as do we, with the private and corporate need for cultural legitimacy and efficacy. We hope you will come away from *UpperDogs* feeling more empowered and truthfully more jazzed about *being* a Christian than you may have before. We hope you will stand a little bit taller, place your steps more confidently and find the adventure of ambassadorship more gripping than ever.

Secondly, our work is unique and it gives us an atypical perspective on what can sometimes feel like time-worn topics of theology and its implementation. Partnership with God takes on different hues when seen through the lens of our curious work.

This book is the second in a series (of sorts). Heather Hughes and I (Sarah Thiessen) run the Splankna Therapy Institute in Denver, Colorado. I was raised in the Church of Christ. I earned an undergraduate degree in Bible and a graduate degree in Marriage and Family Therapy from Abilene Christian University and my plan was to do traditional talk therapy with a national Christian group practice. But the Lord had a different plan. The surprise call on my life has been to redeem for the body of Christ the tools of mind-body psychology. This is a sub-field within the larger field of psychology that uses the same system in the body that acupuncture and chiropractic are based on, to relieve emotional trauma.

This mind-body healing system is based on the arena of science called "quantum" or "subatomic" physics. Up until now, the new age movement has claimed these created mechanisms in the body and subsequently the church has largely disavowed them. God has called the Splankna Institute to be a place where believers can learn how to use this aspect of creation and God's design in it for emotional healing from a biblical basis rather than a secular one. Because of this call and its obvious theological challenges, we've had to ask many unusual questions. We've experienced healing and partnership with God through atypical glasses and it has challenged and enriched our faith in unexpected ways.

Theologically, using mind-body psychology redemptively is no small feat. It requires rigorous clarity and attention to biblical truth and boundaries. Because of that, each of our three levels of training begins with establishing our theology because the truth is always more important than healing. The first book in this series tells the story of how and why I developed Splankna Therapy and then goes through the important spiritual issues that arise in redeeming things that the secular world has attempted to own. Basically, it covers our "theology section" of Level 1 Splankna Training. This book, *UpperDogs*, is our Advanced Training "theology section."

I tell you this for two reasons: one is that there is some overlapping ground to cover such as an encapsulated version of the "redemptive posture" proposed in the first book, and also because throughout our discussion here, we will dip in and out of the world of quantum physics, especially in section 4, exploring that level of creation as a unique reference point that Heather and I bring to the table. When you peek inside an atom, you can't help but emerge as an UpperDog.

But throughout this discussion, Splankna therapy is merely an example of partnership. Whether you're familiar with Splankna or not, the discussion will land in your own backyard. We promise.

UpperDog Christian is meant to operate in two distinct arenas:

1. Cultural Ambassadors
2. Partners with God

However, in both arenas the well-intended Christian can get off balance. When we don't understand who we are, we can fall either into unproductive passivity or aggression. Either way, we mean well. I really believe that. And I'm confident that there is sufficient grace over all of these imbalances. We don't confront these things in order to condemn, but for activation; for the empowerment of the Bride. We love the church. I mean really love the church. Heather and I have both spent our adult lives fighting for her strength and beauty, pouring ourselves into her potential and longing to see her stand tall.

There are things in this book that will be difficult to hear. They were difficult to write. Please ask the Holy Spirit to place his filter over this content as you would with any book. If you notice a strong emotional reaction, stop and ask why. Ask the Spirit to pour a grace over you now so that you can hear whatever pieces are for you. And please know that it's *all* for us. We do not write this from a position of grand arrival but of a continual pressing into what's possible. We've broken things up into four sections:

1. Cultural underdogs (in passivity and aggression)
2. UpperDog Ambassadorship
3. Theological underdogs (in passivity and aggression)
4. UpperDog Partnership.

In the first section we will define how underdog Christianity can end up both in passivity and aggression in dealing with the world and our position in it. The Christian who thinks he's the underdog in the story tends to get off balance. Both cultural passivity and aggression in representing Christianity undermine its strength and beauty. But the truth is that the Christian has the advantage in every way. We have the upper hand as ambassadors of the Hero in the story. We're on the winning team. It is our privilege to deal with our culture from the home-court advantage and it's time we fleshed out what that really means. In order to do that, we need to take an honest look at both our cultural passivity and our cultural aggression. We need to admit the problem in order to craft a solution.

Section two will explore what it might look like to shed both of those imbalances and live in the world around us with the advantage, as the UpperDogs. We'll enjoy a rousing reminder of all the ways we have that advantage: What gives us the upper hand? What's different about the Christian and why is he the Upperdog? What does our advantage consist of? And then we'll explore what it looks like to use it—to navigate through culture in strength and authority as honored, effectual ambassadors of the Hero himself.

In section three and four we will explore the theological side of things. How do we live and operate with God himself? What is the nature of our relationship with the Living God? What is our role in partnering with him? Again, we'll first define the problem. When underdog Christian doesn't understand his role in the story, he errs on the passive or the aggressive side of theology as well. We'll look at passive theology and how it plays out. We'll also admit how we can be aggressive with God and the unproductive fruit of both extremes.

And then our favorite discussion of the book, section four. Here we'll really have some fun. We'll explore productive partnership with God.

We'll look at partnering with him in authority, creativity, obedience and what we call "creative prayer." We'll wonder together about what is *happening* when we pray. We'll discuss the development of faith and its mechanisms. And finally, we'll look into the "how" of partnering with God. Ready?

Section 1

Cultural Underdogs

We'll first explore how both passivity and aggression undermine our effectiveness as cultural ambassadors in this world. Whole books could be written on each of these topics, but here we'll just touch on each one in order to paint a broad picture of the problem because we really want to get to the fun stuff—exploring what it would be like if we lived and moved in our culture with the advantage; as UpperDog Ambassadors.

Cultural Passivity

God, grant that I may never live to be useless.
-John Wesley

Sleeping Dogs Lie

The Underdog Christian doesn't know he's an ambassador of the
Living God. He doesn't realize that he is a representative of the
victor in this story. Subsequently, he doesn't know that he has the
advantage in every situation. This confusion plays out in how he
handles the world around him. He can default into cultural passivity.

On The *De*fense

How does the passive Christian operate in the world? On the
*de*fense. When we don't understand who we are, we can end up
living and moving in our culture as if we're in continual danger,
moving through the secular landscape with our guard up against
contamination. We isolate ourselves from our surroundings in the
attempt to stay clean and safe because we think "their" influence
is greater than ours. We are under-represented at art shows and
concerts, in discussion panels and government seats. We assume
that our arena is small and theirs is large, that most everything
is "worldly" and the pure of heart are relegated to the fringes. It's
when we're intimidated by the girl in the cubicle next door who is

3

a self-proclaimed Wiccan, concerned that she's defiling our corner of the building, but we wouldn't dare speak to her. It's when we pull our children out of public school not to enjoy the gift of teaching, but out of the fear that those "worldly" children will ruin ours. It's when we're intimidated by anything involving "energy" and use "eastern" like a cuss word. We're walking through the world with our shields up.

The defensive posture sees the world as irreparably corrupt. It sees godliness as rare. One night my husband and I were at a small group Bible study. The leader was teaching that an unbeliever is incapable of glorifying God. His reasoning was that since an unbeliever never *intends* to glorify God, he never does. This is an example of underdog thinking. I brought up another point of view. "Think about an Olympic athlete," I suggested. The wondrous strength, precision, dedication and excellence displayed by an elite athlete are all a testimony to the glory of God. All excellence, all beauty, all strength glorifies God whether it means to or not. But underdog thinks that God is only glorified behind stained glass.

Have you ever heard the "origins" argument? It's when the church argues that if something has non-biblical origins then all of its outgrowths are wrong by default. The current hot topic includes all things relating to eastern religions, like yoga or martial arts. These are the kinds of things that the Splankna Institute is actively redeeming. Defensive Christianity assumes that if an individual does not know Jesus as Savior and Lord, he is incapable not only of glorifying God, but of discerning anything true. Underdog Christian thinks that if someone is raised in a Muslim worldview, he cannot search the revealed creation and ascertain accurate information. He assumes that discoveries made by those who don't know Jesus are inaccurate by default. But this is illogical.

This posture consigns God into a very narrow sphere of influence and assumes that the earth is filled with far more lies than truth. But an unbeliever *is* capable of discovering truth. He is capable of correctly observing the creation around him and even deducing correctly from it. It is the Lord God who gives men the ability to reason, to observe, to deduce and he does not give it only to the sanctified. Truth exists in all spheres because it belongs to God and he is holding everything together. We mean well. Our desire is to maintain holiness and rightfully so. We want to make sure we do not become deceived by the conclusions of the ungodly. But righteousness moves into the world, not out of it.

Sometimes we act as if we're the outsiders—like this is the world's party and we're not invited. When passivity takes hold, we live as if the world is comprised of the victors here and we're just hiding out, hoping to go unnoticed. We mill around the sidelines in a defensive trance. We don't go to chiropractors or naturopaths because we're afraid they'll influence us, afraid their darkness will taint us instead of assuming that our presence will change *them.* And if we do dare cross their threshold it's only after several nervous prayers of the "covering" armor of God. While it is an important practice to attend to one's spiritual safety, we must not stop there. This is Christianity on the *De*fense. It is our wrongful assumption that evil is pervasive and godliness sparse. Without even meaning to, we're living like the lost are in the dominant position. But that simply isn't true. We are not the weak ones here. We have the upper hand.

Defeatism

Every week she came to her session and began talking about her issues with the government and her fears of the future. I watched her toil over all these issues that were completely out of her hands.

I see so many people like her on social networking overwhelmed with fears and paranoia because of the direction of our government. Their concerns are legitimate. There are many things happening that are disturbing. But something is out of balance. I wasn't really sure how to process this with my client, so I did the only thing I knew to do—I took it to God in prayer. He revealed the lack of faith in this posture. When we indulge everything from paranoia to conspiracy theorists, we put far too much weight in the government and the things that are wrong with it. We act as though what is happening today is the end-all, the beginning of the end of the world. But the beginning of the end started with Adam and Eve. Throughout history (even in the Bible) people were convinced that the end was near. We must not consider every bad move of the government as our undoing. We cannot allow ourselves to think as if the government and the president have final say. This is another example of our misconception that God is small and something else (government in this case) is bigger.

Part of the key is simply in our focus. When we focus on the negative it will eat us alive. We cannot enjoy the now. We cannot celebrate the victories that we as Christians are making. My son's football team prayed before every game. They worked out to Christian music. My kids have written papers about Jesus being their hero. I hear about people all the time being effective as they do these things, but what makes the news are the moments that are not allowed. Why? I think that we humans like the drama. We love to share the "Can you believe that?" scenarios and the darker the better. Something in our brokenness loves to have that juicy tidbit of dark news, even when it's against our own camp. But when we give in to that temptation, the enemy gets all the attention and the wow. We need to make a conscious choice to give God all of the WOW attention, because an UpperDog knows that God has already won.

The Cat's Got Our Tongue

Another way our passivity can operate is in our silence. When we're together we search the Scriptures. We celebrate the revelation of the Word together but spend years on end in comfortable conversations about football with a co-worker or a neighbor and never mention that Truth. Those conversations are just too anxious. What will they think? I won't be cool and respected anymore. I'll be seen as a nerd, or worse... a *conservative*."

If we say nothing when the boss humiliates someone or a friend lies to his wife or yet another round of gossip is circling through the church, it's because we're more afraid of conflict than we are of God. We don't want to be that way, but it's all too common. Carolyn Arends sings about our silence in her song entitled, "No Trespassing."

> "Nobody asked about the bruises on her face.
> I guess she was glad that they gave her personal space.
> When the bones wouldn't mend and it came to an end
> In the dead of the night
> Well the neighbors were sad
> But at least they had respected her rights.
> We got a new edition to the Golden Rule...
> No Trespassing Allowed."

In recent history, our silence is staggering. How can it be possible that polls show that as many as 75% of Americans claim to be Christians and yet our leaders continue to move away from our historic protection of Israel? How can it be that biblically based Hollywood productions and television mini-series boast the biggest ratings on record but so much of the media that Christians produce is sub-par and campish? Why do we continue to insist on using language in our worship and materials that is detached and archaic? Why are we silent at the pregnant, historical moments like 9/11 where our world cries out for the truth? At best we are baffled and quiet. At worst we are cowering and apologetic of our faith in a God who would allow such travesties, hoping we're not called on to explain him.

Frogs In A Kettle

It was Saturday evening of our church's big annual weekend retreat. We called it "Summit." It was well loved and well attended and on this particular night we were blessed by the wisdom of Mr. Joe Beam. He brought several people up front and had them stand in a line facing the audience with about 10 feet between them. The woman on the far right was to represent "Lucy" from the old sitcom "I Love Lucy." Joe reminisced with the audience about how the producers of that show portrayed Ricky and Lucy as sleeping in separate beds because at that time in American cultural history it would've been considered taboo to portray the intimate aspect of their relationship, even within marriage. Joe then placed a young man just to the right of "Lucy" and said, "This is where the church stood at that time." The church contemporary to Ricky and Lucy looked with mild chagrin on some of the antics and "off color humor" of the show. After all, television is the devil's playground.

Then Joe moved a little to the left in the line and introduced us to "Elvis," whose scandalous pelvic thrusting was far more suggestive than Lucy would've dreamed. The Church stood to the right yet again, aghast and embarrassed. No good Christian teenager would attend an Elvis concert and show her face in Church on Sunday morning. But at this point in history, the church was quite comfortable with Lucy. He stood just to the right of Elvis (a little past Lucy now).

Next to the left was "Archie" from "All In The Family," with his blatant bigotry, misogyny and open sexual humor. Now the church thought Archie was low-brow but come on, Elvis is a classic.

Then we jump to 1981 and the advent of MTV. Here we have not only all forms of sexuality but overt profanity and violence as well. Joe stands the church a foot or two to the right of our MTV star, shunning that downslide in American cultural morality. But he turns to the audience, smiles and says, "But Saturday Night Live is pretty funny, you gotta admit."

He points out that where the church stood in 1981 in its moral compass is a place that even the *world* shunned just a few decades earlier. I sat in the audience that night and I was amazed. I had never noticed that the Church considers herself moral as long as we're a step or two behind culture, no matter where it goes. In our passivity we slowly decay in our own moral standards, feeling righteous all the while because we're not quite as bad as the world around us. We sedate ourselves with our relative righteousness. In 1950 even the atheist considered shameful things like divorce and unwed pregnancy. But now the church begins to welcome homosexuality in leadership and rarely blinks at divorce. The heat of degradation rises so slowly that we don't even realize we're boiling to death.

Everything's Fine

Another way our cultural passivity rears its ugly head is in our denial of the desperate need in our world. This is one of the ways where I struggle the most. One of my greater weaknesses is in my tendency to forget about the lost. Having grown up in the church and spending my life surrounded by fellow believers, I can easily pretend that everybody's O.K., that there isn't a sea of captives all around me bound to a terrible fate. I've always had such a love for the church—so much passion to see her rise up in strength and joy. But my love for the world, my compassion for the lost, is weak. It's one of the biggest ways I fight with my own inner underdog.

But we don't just ignore the lost in our passivity. We can also be guilty of ignoring the need itself. In James 1:27 "true religion" is defined as the active caring for widows and orphans. While we do attend to this vein of Christianity through amazing organizations like Samaritan's Purse and Habitat for Humanity, we make an unnecessarily small dent in the global desperation considering our collective resources.

There are so many ways that our passivity disempowers our message. We are meant to be light and salt in this world. Both are active. Remember the parable of the talents in Matthew and Luke? When we choose passivity we are representing the poor guy with the single talent. When given his task, he was afraid. He was afraid both of his own lack of competence and of the judgment of his master. He reasoned that the best course of action would be to bury his talent and keep it "safe" for his master. Quintessential passivity. He chose fear and laid low. He protected what was entrusted to him and had it to give back to the master on that fateful day. But it did not go well for him. Protecting our own faith and righteousness is not what we're here for. The other two servants did something productive with what was entrusted to them. Something productive outside of themselves. They went beyond passive protection into action, into multiplication. Because of them the Master returned to his estate in literal, measurable improvement. But the one who merely protected himself was cursed. On that day, our personal faith well-preserved is not going to be any more pleasing to our Master than his buried talent. What good is an ambassador who stays in his own country?

Cultural Aggression

"I like your Christ, I do not like your Christians.
Your Christians are so unlike your Christ."
- Mahatma Gandhi

It's clear how cultural passivity can work against us as ambassadors. But underdog Christianity can also err in the opposite direction: ungodly aggression. When we don't understand our position in the world and with God, we can fall into passivity, yes, but also into *over*-compensation. This manifests in several ways. Without a solid understanding of our ambassadorship in the world, we can fall into elitism, judgmentalism, scare tactics and even violence.

Dog Eat Dog

The aggressive underdog refuses to celebrate Christmas because it's a "pagan holiday." He scorns the Easter bunny and any church body that would stoop to hunting eggs. He assumes that if it's got a heavy backbeat it's probably trashy and cries, "Show me Scripture and verse!" whenever he's challenged. His bumper sticker reads, "If it ain't King James, it ain't Bible," and the list of things he's against is far longer than the list of what he's for. He reviles a worship band and is certain that no one in that service is truly worshipping. He wouldn't dare cut a rug or have a glass of champagne to toast the New Year or his daughter's wedding. He can't believe that the men's group at that other church has poker night every other Wednesday and he thinks the only sermon worth hearing is a strict reminder of one's sin. He knows that people who raise their hands in praise are just looking for attention and that all speaking in tongues is fake and sensational. (He actually thinks it's demonic but he won't usually say that out loud.) He's certain that "the saints" are few and far between and he's sure glad to be in that number.

These overcompensations into aggression may seem like fierce devotion, but they miss the fact that we're representing a God who "is love."[5] When we don't understand who we are in Christ, that we already have the upper hand, we can end up acting like a bully on a playground—forcefully putting down everyone else in order to make ourselves feel better. Or in this case, feel *right*.

I was cleaning up the registration table at one of our training conferences when a businessman approached and asked me about Splankna. I began by explaining to him that Splankna is Christian mind-body psychology. I talked about how we had developed our protocol from a biblical perspective. He bristled up and stopped me. "I'm an atheist," he announced gruffly. I could tell from his protective tone and posture that he was prepared for a negative and aggressive approach to this admission. My response was not at all what he was accustomed to. I said "Oh that's okay, this protocol is effective for all God's children, whether or not they believe in him."

The longer we talked the more he disclosed his opinion of Christians. In his experience Christians usually attempt to threaten and strong-arm him into believing in God. Their aggression undermined the credibility of a loving God. As we talked it became obvious that he yearned for a motivation to believe. He wanted me to convince him. It wasn't that he didn't believe in God, he most certainly did, he just thought of God as a jerk. He was adamant that he wasn't interested in worshipping the God that he thought was real—an angry, selfish God. He was longing for a God of love and mercy.

When we come from a position that lacks love and mercy, we are missing the point of who God is. Upon returning from a mission trip in Uganda, with our two older boys who were 10 and 12 at the time, the church asked us to speak about our experience. They wanted to know what we were taking away from such a trip. I asked the boys to pray and write about how the trip to Uganda impacted their views in life. Both of them said some profound things. I don't remember Ethan's exact speech but I vividly remember the end. He said, "I believe we are all disciples of someone, but the question is, of who?" We can learn a lot from this 10 year old. His point, of course, was that we are all being led and influenced by someone. Who is your example? Jesus is the one who picked up the woman caught in sin and said, "...neither do I condemn you."[6]

In Switchfoot's song, "Dare You To Move," they sing about how everyone is watching, everyone waits on us. They sing about how there is a tension between who we are and who we could be. What kind of example do you want to be? When we approach the world with the aggressive threatening posture, we are not a reflection of Christ. God is not being represented in his true nature. God isn't seen as loving, he is seen as hard, removed, judgmental and manipulative.

People may follow that God out of fear, but they won't know his love. They won't truly love him, therefore their loyalty is fragile. There are plenty of Christians living in this version of religion. Unfortunately they are suffering without cause. Jesus said he came to set the captives free, but condemnation is captivity.

Silver Swords And White Sheets

Very unfortunately, one of the most common things that discredits Christianity in the eyes of the world is our blood-stained socio-political history. Shameful examples like religious endorsement of slavery, violent acts against abortion clinics and the Ku Klux Klan are glaring examples. But righteous violence is not God's design for how we are to represent him in this world. Hate crimes are not holy. Of course there is a place and time for the sword. But there is nothing about bombing an abortion clinic or a gay rights parade that advances the Kingdom.

I had never felt anything like it before. I was praying with a client about a generational stronghold that involved violence in the name of the Lord. As we walked through confession and repentance on behalf of the bloodline, I suddenly felt an enormous weight come down over my back. With that weight came an intense feeling of offense. I knew it was not my own. God allowed me, just for a moment or two, to feel some of his own offense at violence having been done in his name. It was remarkable and sobering. I've never forgotten it. It showed me some of the fierceness of the God I tend to see in an overly cozy light. Paradoxically, God shows his most stern side in response to aggressive religion. Jesus' most scathing remarks were to the religious leaders who were hostile and condemning towards his people.

In-Fighting

Paul is exasperated. You can hear the frustration in his voice as he tries to reason with the Corinthian church. He cries, "The very fact that you have lawsuits among you means you have been completely defeated already! Why not rather be wronged? Why not rather be cheated?"[7] When we fight with each other over trivial issues or even significant ones, we undermine our ambassadorship in the world.

Jesus said that it would be "by our love" that they would know we are Christians. The world around us is well aware of our internal squabbling. They love to put it on the nightly news along with the sin of every visible pastor. But when we love each other, when we handle our differences in mutual respect and blessing, we represent him well and the world takes notice.

Steve Bond writes: "In the late 1800's there were two deacons in a small Baptist church in Mayfield, Kentucky. These two deacons didn't get along and they always opposed each other in any decision related to the church. On one particular Sunday, one deacon put up a small wooden peg in the back wall so the minister could hang up his hat. When the other deacon discovered the peg, he was outraged that he had not been consulted. People in the church took sides and eventually there was a spilt. To this day, they say you can find in Mayfield, the Anti-Peg Baptist Church." [8] One of the most common accusations against Christianity is "hypocrisy." When we fight with each other we deserve that reputation. Our bickering contradicts our message. It misrepresents the Gospel and God himself. Think of how you feel when your children act like banshees in public. God can relate.

Scare Tactics

Looking back on it, I can't believe how much allowance we had as children. The world was a different place in the 70's. And I grew up in Los Angeles! My friend Valerie Schmidt and I would walk home from fourth grade together across several five-lane city streets. Valerie wasn't a believer and I distinctly remember long, conscientious conversations with her about her language. I spent many a hot, smoggy, afternoon walk trying to help her understand that if she continued to curse, she would go to hell. (I really did.) I wasn't much different from the hell fire and brimstone preachers of the early 1900's. When we think our greatest leverage with a dying world is to threaten them as "sinners in the hands of an angry God," we're operating as aggressive underdogs. God does not long for a sea of terrified hell-escapees. Fear is not our leverage, love is. Only the underdog needs to resort to threats.

We play this same card in another way: paranoid eschatology. These are the Christians who have heralded every president since Truman as the probable Anti-Christ. They own several copies of "The Late Great Planet Earth" and check in daily with the political happenings in Israel, not out of a deep love for God's nation but in order to find the next clue to imminent Armageddon. Rumination on all the expected horrors of the coming tribulation is another way we play the underdog. We have extrapolated volumes of coming doom from mysterious, symbolic Scriptures and wear our terror as a badge of spiritual realism. But living on eschatological adrenaline is not taking the upper hand.

Even if the partial preterists are wrong and the future holds the worst-case scenario, the focus was never meant to be on fear but on dominion and the advancement of the Kingdom. Prophesies were given not to make us tremble but to embolden us. Underdog is deceived into thinking that obsessing over the "end times" makes him prepared. He thinks he's following the scriptural injunction to "keep watch."[9] But again, things are off balance. The retort comes, "I'm not afraid, I'm just aware." But that's the very ruse of all paranoia: "This is your safety," when really it's your trap. Over-focus on potential evil does not stave it off. It does not give you greater peace and protection, only greater fear.

Downward Dog

So why are we like this? What are the makings of an underdog Christian? There are many reasons why we play the underdog. Good old-fashioned guilt is one of them. Our stubborn guilt and shame can lock us into underdog status. For illustration, let's visit David just after the Bathsheba scandal.

After Nathan approached David and told him the disconcerting parable of the sheep, David was sincerely convicted. He confessed his iniquity before God. God forgave him and he suffered the consequences of his sin by losing his baby. Did you ever notice the change in David? He was never the same. You can see it later in how he handles things with Absalom, Amnon, and Tamar in 2 Samuel. When Absalom came to his father David and requested justice to be served in the case of Amnon raping his sister Tamar, David did nothing. Nothing! It's as if he thought to himself, "Who am I to condemn Amnon after what I did with Bathsheba?"

If David had been able to accept forgiveness and release the guilt of his sin, he might have been able to confront the sin that Amnon committed. He might have brought a level of peace to Absalom. But because he chose to do nothing, Absalom was overcome with anger and vengeance, which he eventually carried out. David lost two sons instead of one. You can witness his grief in 2 Samuel 19:4 "The king covered his face and cried aloud, 'O my son Absalom! O Absalom, my son, my son!'" Guilt had paralyzed him and kept him the underdog and now he would suffer for it.

When my son was very young, I made him a little teddy bear out of scrap material. The material was an antique-looking army green. It wasn't eye-catching but I thought it would make an adorable teddy bear. I embroidered his initials in the teddy bear and I gave it to him with joyful anticipation. He took one look at it and with disgust in his eyes he let me know in no uncertain terms that he didn't like it and he didn't want it. Feeling dejected, I did not do an adequate job of hiding my disappointment. I knew he was young and without a filter, so I decided not to take it personally. I told him not to worry about it and that he could have it if he changed his mind. Later that day, he felt convicted about hurting my feelings and he apologized. We had a great talk and all was forgiven.

Months later he came to me with his bear in hand and guilt in his heart and he apologized again. He hugged the bear and told me that he loved it and he would keep it forever. To be honest, I hadn't even remembered it until he brought it up. I comforted him in his guilt and we worked it out again. I thought to myself, "What a sweet boy." Then a few months later, the same scene happened. With a wrinkled forehead, I pondered for a while, what's going on here? Then I began to notice a pattern; every time he saw the bear he would come to me in guilt and apologize again. This wasn't a sweet gesture, this was stubborn guilt.

This story made me think of our God who chooses to remember our sins no more, yet we bring them up over and over. Why couldn't my son let go of the guilt and accept the forgiveness that I offered? Why can't we let go of guilt and accept the sacrifice Jesus offered? Stubborn guilt is not from God. God brings conviction not guilt. Conviction inspires you to greater righteousness. Guilt is the counterfeit to God's conviction. It is the enemy's condemnation. How do you know the difference? God's conviction inspires you to greater holiness. It draws you upward. The enemy's condemnation is like a big black thumb, squashing you down into self-hatred. It is filled with hopeless and shaming messages. It pushes you downward.

Is there guilt that you are holding on to? Are you allowing condemnation in the name of holiness? At some point you'll need to reject it. You'll need to truly surrender it to Jesus in order to overcome your inner underdog. You cannot live like an UpperDog in this world while you're dragging around a lifetime of wrongs. They're like huge rocks in your backpack and they're wrinkling your cape.

Such A Worm As I

Mary Esther had lived 92 years in faith by the time this exchange occurred. She was my grandmother and the namesake of my oldest daughter. In 1945, she had a daughter, twin boys and was pregnant with another set of twins when her husband contracted Hodgkin's Lymphoma. When her two new baby girls were still infants she lost her husband and was all on her own. She held on to her love for the Lord as she started two businesses to support herself and her children. She was always a pillar in her church and in her community. She raised five children, who produced many children and grandchildren, all who are walking in faith today. She was no more perfect than anyone else, but she lived her entire life trusting Jesus.

I was hugging her goodbye, her iconic silver bun pressing against my cheek. Her body was becoming frail enough that she could be meeting the Lord any day. "Love you. See you next year," I said. She dropped her gaze and said feebly, "I hope so." "Well," I said, "If I don't see you here, I'll see you at an even better party!" At this, she looked down once again, and instead of perking up with that wonderful reality, she repeated, "Well, I hope so."

"Grandma!" I said with shock. "Don't you dare say that!" "You know very well where you're going," I scolded. After a lifetime of trusting the Lord and following him she was standing at the precipice of the next chapter hanging her head. This was not an example of godly humility, but of a false understanding of the gospel and of who she was. As George McDonald said, "We remain such creeping Christians because we look at ourselves instead of Christ." Godly humility is responding to the glory in oneself with deep gratefulness and privilege because of the awareness that all of it is really credited to the Lord. It is based in gratefulness, in joy, not in shame. Her false humility in that moment was not a credit to Jesus. It was an unwitting rejection of him and the fullness of his accomplishment on her behalf. And the most amazing part of it all is that Jesus' same accomplishment covers even her imbalance. Today, with him, she finally really knows it.

In 2 Samuel we find another example of false humility in Jonathon's son Mephibosheth. Now it was a common practice at that time for the new king to annihilate the relatives of the previous king. But David treasured his friend Jonathon. He made an oath not to abolish his lineage. David is actually looking to bless and honor anyone who is left in the house of Jonathon so he calls on Mephibosheth. But Mephibosheth is anticipating what's typical. David says to him, "Don't be afraid, for I will surely show you kindness for the sake of your father Jonathan. I will restore to you all the land that belonged to your grandfather Saul and you will always eat at my table." This act of grace and generosity was unheard of. Mephibosheth replied, "Why would you notice a dead dog like me?"

The underdog is like that with God. We don't deserve, in our own right, a position in the Kingdom. We don't deserve to sit at the king's table. Yet, Jesus says, "Come and reign with me." We say, "No not me, I'm not worthy. I don't have what it takes to represent you in this world." In the name of humility we are actually embracing condemnation. Do we think we see ourselves more accurately than he does?

Underdog Fears Conflict

Our social fears are another factor in our cultural underdog status. What are you afraid of when you don't stand up for yourself or someone else? Are you afraid of breaking a relationship with the culprit? Recently we had a controversy at my children's school. At the board meeting I could tell that God was prompting me to be an opposing voice. He wanted me to say what needed to be heard by so many. As the antagonist in the issue was speaking, I could feel my heart beating faster and stronger. The whole time I was praying for the Holy Spirit to lead and speak through me.

When they called on me, I went with the prompting and I said the things that no one else was willing to say. In the middle of my little speech a loud noise erupted and scared me. It was then I realized that everyone was clapping. Afterward, many people thanked me for saying what they felt, but hadn't said. I had to let go of comfortable silence. It was a time to fight for the weak ones, the ones who were scared or unable to speak.

It would have been easy to choose passivity in that situation. To think, "What business is it of mine? Who am I to tell the parents that they should be ashamed of themselves for gossiping and making the issue more traumatic then it already was? What gives me the right to stand up for the teachers and staff?" But the truth is that I not only have a right but a responsibility. We all do. What are we afraid of? Are we afraid those parent's won't like us? So what if they don't? I knew as soon as I was done speaking that I had made some enemies that day. If we really sat down with fear and said, "OK, so what is it that I'm afraid of," we'd probably be a lot less passive when we realize how insignificant those fears really are.

He Fears Abandonment

He was a leader in a fairly legalistic church. As he grew in relationship with God, he learned the difference between rules and love. He could no longer be a part of a church with such legalistic views on music, women in leadership, and the Holy Spirit's interaction. He started a new church, a church that would follow the Bible and let the Holy Spirit lead. It was a great church, more like the original ones we read about in the Bible. But there was a problem. Some of the other leaders in the new church wanted to pick and choose which legalist rules they wanted to keep. He thought he was keeping the peace by agreeing with them. He decided to just give in on an issue or two rather than cause waves. For instance, he decided not have the women take active roles in the church. "Then everyone will be happy" he thought to himself. Really? Everyone?

What about the women who are not allowed to use their gifts within the church? They feel forsaken and irrelevant. They are forced to wonder if maybe they are inferior. They feel limited in the Kingdom and trapped by the leaders' passivity. When avoiding conflict is our highest goal, we become impotent and peace is still not achieved. Any church leader knows it's impossible to please everyone. Fear of conflict cannot be our compass or the battle is over before it starts.

When passivity reigns, the church becomes ineffectual in so many areas. It's no wonder the world doesn't have more respect for the church. Brennan Manning said, "The greatest single cause of atheism in the world today is Christians who acknowledge Jesus with their lips and walk out the door and deny Him by their lifestyle."[10] Passivity is one of the subtle ways we deny him. Scripture talks about this in Romans 1:32 "Although they know God's righteous decree that those who do such things deserve death, they not only continue to do these very things but also approve of those who practice them."

We talked about Joe Beam's analogy of how the church is always one step behind the cultural norm and we think that makes us holy. What it makes us is a willow in the wind. We sway with the culture and the times. There is still such a thing as right and wrong. We need to have a faith that we can be proud of—a faith that stands up and says, "No more!" to culturally accepted sin. UpperDog isn't afraid to step on a few toes. He's willing to turn over tables.

EgoDog

We've discussed some of the deep reasons why we lean toward passivity. But why do we lean towards the aggressive side of things? Ego plays a big part. Sometimes there's just some basic human pride involved and pride often leads to aggression. Pride is such a universal temptation that Satan even tried to hook Jesus with it. "The devil took him to a very high mountain and showed him all the kingdoms of the world and their splendor. 'All this I will give you'" (Matthew 4:8-9). Why be a humble king who lets people choose to worship you, when you can be grand, spectacular and irresistible in the eyes of the whole world? Jesus didn't fall for it, but sometimes we do.

Everyone wants respect and approval. It's correct to seek the approval of God. We yearn to hear those words, "Well done good and faithful servant,"[11] and rightfully so. It's when we're bound to the approval of man that we get messed up, and we're more bound to it than we realize. "Pride goes before destruction, a haughty spirit before a fall."[12] At times I have almost felt controlled by prideful urges. I couldn't relax in church and worship God because I couldn't stop thinking about what people think of me. If I put my hands up do they think I'm doing it to be showy? What if the people in front of me hear me singing out of tune? I want to shout at myself, "Alright already! Let it go!" I want to be free to worship without thinking about what everyone around me is thinking.

Once during a fast I learned to close my eyes and imagine that it was just Jesus and me. I have this secret with Jesus: when I move into worship I close my eyes and I say, "It's just you and me on the dance floor." In my imagination everyone else fades away and I don't have to concern myself with what they think. It's just the two of us.

The management of pride can take effort. We can be so overcome with ourselves that we miss what matters. The worst part is that whatever we are most focused on is what we are truly worshiping. If I'm focused on my image, then my image is what I'm truly worshiping. We can fall into aggression with the world when we're a little too impressed with ourselves.

Instead of being able to see ourselves clearly, we look at our brother and say, "Well, at least I don't do what he does," or "I would never be that big of a hypocrite." "His sin is simply deplorable but mine doesn't really count." This attitude is what Jesus is combatting when he talks about lust being the same as sexual sin and anger being the same as murder.[13] We have to admit it—pride is an issue. Even Jesus' own disciples, (who should've been feeling quite sufficiently validated), are found fighting for the right to be second in command when Jesus comes into power.[14]

Lone Rangers

The Aggressive underdog is going it alone and he's going to do it his way. At some point he starts thinking, "what do I need God for?" He starts believing he's self-sufficient. Or maybe he just never thought of God's involvement as literal in his life. You wouldn't believe how commonly I'll be in session with a believing client who's pouring out some pain or dilemma or important life decision before me. I listen carefully and then ask what appears to me the most obvious question: "What do you get when you ask God about it?" The client stares at me in an uncomfortable pause before answering, "Well, I haven't asked God." Really?

Another way this theology of self-sufficiency plays out is when we try to bully the world into faith because we think it's all up to us. We have to shame or scare them into believing because God is just watching. We're not trusting that he's drawing them already.

Sometimes its simply pride that turns us toward self-sufficiency. But even God doesn't choose to be self-sufficient. God has chosen to be dependent on us. He chose to create partners whose contribution actually counts. "If my people would only pray...."[15] He created a world where we get to reign with him. Why in the world do we strive for independence when our perfect creator offers partnership? He is omnipotent and yet he allows us to be a part of the story. He bids us come and knock. He invites us to ask.

Yet we have a tendency to be like rebellious teenagers. We think we have it all figured out. We have no patience to wait on God. We get so prideful that we think we know the answer before we even ask the question. It's frustrating sometimes when I get a prayer request from someone and they are basically telling me to join them in forcing God to do their will.

The morning of 9/11 had a major impact on everyone. I remember watching the news as a million thoughts raced through my head. I was especially focused on my little brother, Nick. He was in the military and I was terrified. I am really close to my siblings. When I was young my mom had to work long, hard hours to provide for the family. I slipped into the mommy role. I was seven when Nick was born and I've always loved him like he was my own child. Nick makes everyone feel welcome and loved. We've had many deep conversations and I know his heart. On 9/11, I was terrified of war. I was afraid my brother would be killed or at the very least changed into an unrecognizable person. I prayed night and day for Nick. I didn't want him to have any part in this war. When Nick was deployed I felt like God hadn't answered that prayer. I was sick over it. I couldn't sleep. When Nick left, I had no faith that God would protect him. After all, he let him go in the first place. I couldn't see any way that this could be God's best for Nick. If only God would have listened to me and done it my way.

During one of my sleepless nights God led me to the kitchen with my Bible. I made a cup of hot tea, and for the first time, I felt a little bit of peace. It felt like God was in the kitchen with me at 2 a.m. and we were having tea together. Then he led me to Psalm 34, "I sought the Lord and he answered me; he delivered me from all my fears." "Blessed is the one who takes refuge in him." "He protects all his bones, not one of them will be broken." Over and over this chapter was God showing me, "I've got him." My eyes were opened. I was convicted that I had been prideful in thinking I knew what was best for Nick. I had been trying to persuade God to do it my way. Through this chapter, I realized that God was with him and that God was taking care of him.

Then God taught me how to pray for Nick. Instead of being paralyzed because God had "obviously" abandoned Nick (and me in the process). I began to pray that the deployment would bring him a deeper reliance on God. I prayed that he would not see or experience anything that would change him. I fasted for him. I felt much more like a partner with God. It's amazing what we can do when we partner instead of rebel. To this day, I have never seen fruit from my rebellion on any topic. Imagine that!

Sometimes when I think about how prideful and demanding we are I have to laugh. Who do we think we are? Why do we think we need to demand anything from God? Could you imagine the mass chaos if he actually gave us everything we demanded? The Hollywood blockbuster, *Bruce Almighty* did a great job of exploring that idea. Did you see it? Jim Carrey's character, "Bruce" has temporarily been given all of God's power. Bruce thinks that God is screwing things up and that he could do better, so God gives him a chance to run things himself. As Bruce receives prayer requests from people, he answers each one with an instant "Yes!" As a result, massive mayhem ensues. Tidal waves and tsunami's roar, the economy collapses due to everyone winning the lottery and riots break out all around. "Yes," is not always the most loving answer.

One of the fundamental problems with "Word of Faith" thinking is the assumption that we know what should happen in any given circumstance. When God responds to Job in chapter 38, he goes on for four chapters listing the amazing things he has done that we had no part in: "Who is this that darkens MY counsel with words without knowledge? Where were you when I laid the earth's foundations? Who provides food for the raven?" etc., etc. There is something about God's response to Job that makes me feel safe and awed at the same time.

So...

So we've defined the problem of the underdog Christian as he operates culturally through the frame of passivity and aggression. Now let's look at how UpperDog operates in the secular arena. What might it look like to be a Productive Ambassador of the Living God in the world?

Section 2

UpperDog Ambassadors

*"Christianity is not to be stinted in her
giving. She is not to be a beggar.
She is to be a giver. She has something from heaven
to give that the world does not have."*
-John G. Lake

So now that we've established underdog Christian's error, let's paint a better picture. What would it look like to really embrace the reality that we are the legitimate ambassadors of the King of it all? What would we have to wrap our heads around in order to operate like powerful cultural Ambassadors?

Love 4 Wins

UpperDog has to start with the basics. He has to have his feet grounded in the reality that God's impact in the world is much larger than the worst evil. It's one of the most fundamental places he must begin in order to take hold of the upper hand. He must know that he represents the winner in this story... the Hero.

Have you seen the bumper sticker, *Love Wins*? Best motto ever. Love does most definitely win. But we tend to think of that only in terms of Heaven. We do expect love to win—eventually—but we don't think of love as winning currently. We look around our world and think that right now, love is losing. Evil looks really big. Governments pass laws against faith. Statistics on horrors like world hunger, child sex trafficking and murder rates are constantly bombarding us. Sexual immorality, drug abuse, false religion and general societal debauchery feel like they're taking over. It looks like the "prince of the air" is having a heyday and gaining momentum as we speak. But is he really?

I want to suggest a different perspective. Remember how God created all that is and then stood back to survey it? As he looked over all that he made, he exclaimed, "It is good." I contend that his opinion has not changed. He says in Romans 1:20 that man has "no excuse" not to acknowledge his existence and his role as creator. Man has only to look to his right or left to see indisputable evidence both of

God's presence and his goodness. Or, as G.K. Chesterton put it, "The world will never starve for want of wonders."[16] C.S. Lewis said, "A man can no more diminish God's glory by refusing to worship him than a lunatic can put out the sun by scribbling 'darkness' on the walls of his cell."[17]

When God looks at this world, surely he sees all that we see. Surely he realizes all the mounting evil. He knows we sin and are sinned against almost constantly. And yet he unapologetically commands us to be joyful! He even goes so far as to ask us to "give thanks in all circumstances."[18] Seriously God? All circumstances? Uh, hello? Do you see what's going on down here? Of course he sees it, but he sees *more* of it than we do. He sees more *in* it than we do. He sees that even in the gravest evil circumstance or individual, there lies far more life than death, far more of his own mark than that of the evil one.

Let's look at an example. Let's take the most evil individual we can think of, like a mass murderer, or Attila the Hun, or our favorite cliché example, Hitler. If you considered just this individual as a whole, and measured him for both his glory and his evil, how much of God does he represent, and how much of the devil? If you tallied it all up, what you would find is that even the vilest human being represents vastly more of God than Satan. Stay with me here. Yes, this person has chosen great sin and caused great harm. But look at him for a minute. Standing there, he still is, regardless of his sin, a representative of God's own image. He has faculties that are marvelous and unsearchable beyond understanding. He has the ability to think, feel, choose, reign, move and develop. He can create and destroy. He has self-awareness. He can love. He can worship. And all of this with opposable thumbs!

Look at just his physiology for a moment. Are you ready for this? Our super evil guy can *see*! I mean, he has these two little water-filled balls, stuck in his face, that somehow mysteriously reflect light and project images into his skull! Once these little balls project those images, he has this incredible thing called a brain that can actually interpret these images and make sense of them! He's amazing! With all of our grand advancements in science and medicine we still have no idea how a human being actually sees. Did you know that? Just a working eyeball represents vast, intricate glory. A working eyeball is a marvelous revelation of goodness and grace.

You know what else about this evil guy? He can breathe! I'm serious! He has these things called lungs that somehow know how to draw in oxygen from his environment, absorb that oxygen and then use it to keep the rest of his body alive! Really! You wouldn't believe it! And his crowning glory? He can *reason*! He can independently navigate a life, make choices, reign over his world. He's an astonishing specimen. Every move he makes is a marvel beyond explanation. He's literally reeking with the glory of God.

Now let's get even crazier. Let's look at just the sum of his *behavior* and see how that tally comes out. In order to perform any behavior he has to make choices. How many choices has this guy made in his lifetime? Billions? What did most of them consist of? We know about the *famous* choices he's made… the ones that have earned him the title of our evil test sample and got him on the nightly news. But those add up to probably about .001% of his total choices. The vast majority of his choices were the natural kind, the kind we're designed by God to make. He chose to tie a shoe, to go to bed, to brush his hair. He chose things like whether or not to eat an apple (no pun intended). And you know there had to be times, even if they were very few, when he did choose a kind word, a courteous action, a smile. No human being is capable of pure, constant sin. Yes, our *state* of fallenness is constant, but its expression is not. Even in his spectacular evil-ness, the sum of his behavior still represents more of God's design than the enemy's. As we tally up our best case example of evil, God still comes out ahead. Way ahead. As our subject stands before our evaluation, the fingerprint of God calls out from his every buzzing, quantum particle. He is mystery and beauty beyond explanation.

Now of course, I'm not saying our guy is saved, just because he's still more of a representation of God than the enemy. But salvation was never about our goodness. The saved are not so categorized because their tally comes out on the plus side. It is only the perfect score of Jesus himself resting on us that saves us. But saved or not, evil-man still represents more of God than anything else.

Love is *currently* winning.

I know it doesn't always feel that way. I have personally had many times in my life when I was unable to hold on to that reality, when the pain and evil of this life, or even from within me, got the upper hand in the moment. But even when I can't feel it, love is still winning. Even if it seems harsh at times, we "have no excuse" for thinking differently. UpperDog knows that love is already winning, and he holds on to it as both a lifeline and a victory cry. It is the wind in his cape.

Christians Have The Advantage

In Chapters 1-4 we beat ourselves up a bit. Now let's refresh the soul. Let's remember what *gives* us the upper hand. If we're going to live like UpperDogs, we need to train our hearts in the biblical actuality. We need to really investigate our position in this world. As ambassadors of the Kingdom of God, as sidekicks to the Hero, we have the advantage in every aspect.

Our Team Has ...
> The Creator
> The Love
> The Wisdom
> The Truth
> The Resources
> The Comfort
> The Hope
> The Joy
> The Authority
> The Life
> The Victory
> The Holy Spirit
> The Power

This status gives us the automatic advantage in any room. If we really wrapped our minds around these realities, we would be transformed. So now let's have some fun. Let's swim around happily in all that's true for a moment. Let's remember who we are. Let's explore a few of these advantages afforded us on the winning team. Once these get pounded a little deeper into our UpperDog psyches, we can start to move differently in our culture. No passivity, no aggression, just productive ambassadorship. The Christian walks into any room with the deck stacked in his favor. All the good stuff is already ours!

The Creator

Let's discuss good and evil. How's that for a segue? One of the things that keeps us underdogs is confusion about this most basic issue. What is good and what is evil? We've already mentioned how we're largely known for what we *don't* do. We're known for what we condemn and avoid. The world holds a myriad of options in behavior and experience and what makes a Christian is the percentage of those that he refuses to engage in because of his God who says "No."

Last Sunday my family and I went to church with my husband's parents. We had heard about the new preacher at this mega-church and we were not disappointed. He was riveting, bald and dressed like a gen-x-er. His main point was that we see God's laws as prison bars when we should be seeing them as guardrails. He warned us that he was going to "step on toes" and talked about sexuality. God's law says sex belongs only inside of marriage and we see that as painfully restrictive, like following God keeps you from all the fun. This preacher established in brilliant articulation that this is a perfect example of God's laws really being guardrails—put in place because he knows what will most bless us, not because he's a party pooper. His laws are not restriction, they're protection, kindness.

Great point. Love it. Absolutely true. Now let's move even further.

If we stop there, we're still thinking small. Yes, righteous living is for our benefit, not our restriction. Avoid sin for your own blessing. But there is even more ground to cover. Let's grow out of a theology of sin management as its highest aim. It's time to move past thinking that the Christian life is about what we avoid and that our greatest goal is purity alone. We must learn to think like contributors. We must learn to think *redemptively.* The redemptive posture recognizes that all things the enemy does or uses have their root in God. Satan cannot create. Everything evil is a mere distortion of some Godly core. If we believe the Genesis account, then this has to be true. When God looked out over his creation he did not say: "Well, I did my best. I guess it's mostly good, but those sections over there are evil." No, he called it *all* good. So unless there's another creator *x nihilo*, all things evil had to start by taking something God created as good and morphing it into a perverted form. The only lie that's effective is the one that's mostly true. UpperDog recognizes that everything belongs to God in its origin, even if mining that origin takes a little elbow grease.

Sex is still a perfect example. If you were dropped into our world, a sentient yet completely naïve human being, would you look around and conclude that sexuality is pure and godly? Definitely not. What our world has done with sexuality, not only now but in different forms throughout human history, is far from God's design. And yet as believers we don't "throw the baby out with the bathwater" so to speak. We retain the clarity that no matter how currently perverted, sexuality, at its core, is of God. We actively redeem it. We take it back on purpose, clean it up and praise God for it.

Let's look at another example; something we clearly see as evil—witchcraft. Scripture repeatedly condemns witchcraft as evil, right? Why then are there so many places in Scripture where God either commands or endorses the same physical structures that witchcraft uses? In Numbers 21[19] he instructs Moses to put a snake on a stick. He tells the people that if they look at the snake, they will be cured from their terminal illness. God instructs a man with leprosy to dip seven times in the river in order to be healed,[20] and Jesus puts mud on someone's eyes.[21] Aaron's staff buds[22] and Moses's staff turns into a snake[23]. Jeremiah is instructed to break some pottery as part of a devastating proclamation against Israel.[24] Only if Moses' hands stay up in the air do the Israelites keep winning the battle in Exodus 17. If you hadn't heard these biblical accounts, and someone told you about them out of context, they would sound an awful lot like witchcraft. And yet, these are examples of the instructions of God. How can that be?

How? Because even in witchcraft, the reason the particular structures are used, such as spell, amulet, incantation, etc. is because those structures have power, they carry weight to effect things. The only reason that could be, based on Genesis 1:30, is that God *made* them to be effective. They could only "work" and be useful for evil purposes if God infused them with efficacy for *his* purposes originally. Evil merely pilfers something God created to be powerful and effective and uses it for rebellious purposes. Make no mistake; witchcraft is evil. The rebelliousness in it is evil and so is the way witchcraft uses God's structures. But everything evil has a Godly core that's been distorted. Everything.

Have you ever noticed that no one bothers to counterfeit a $3.00 bill? Why not? Because it wouldn't be a useful deception. It wouldn't work. Nobody would be tricked. It only makes sense to create a counterfeit of something legitimate. Counterfeit a $100 bill and you're getting somewhere. Everything the enemy counterfeits began with something legitimate or else he wouldn't bother.

The Splankna Therapy Institute's stomping ground of redemption in new age thinking is another example. New age philosophy is a collection of lies that are mostly true. For instance:

New Ages Says	Biblical basis	Lie	Truth
"You have the divine spark within you."	"We are the temple of the living God."[25] And, "Let us make man in our own image."[26]	You are equal with God. He is not a distinct being. You *are* god.	You are made in his image. You have qualities like him that the rest of creation does not have.
"God is just the great animating principle of the universe… the nebulous, organizing force without personhood."	"All things are from him and through him and to him."[27] and that, "He sustains all things by his powerful word."	God is in everything, therefore you are god and so is the rock and the tree.	God does animate and sustain all things. He also remains distinct from His creation, hierarchically above it and sovereign over it.

There is a true, redeemable core in lies like these. That's why they're effective. (For a broader discussion on redemptive posture toward new age thinking, please check out the first book, *Splankna: The Redemption of Energy Healing for the Kingdom of God.*)[28]

This paradigm shift is a good place to start building UpperDog muscles. The Creator's declaration is either true or it isn't. It is either all good, or it's not. Evil is a distortion, an aberration only, not a legitimate chunk of creation in and of itself. Everything everywhere is rightfully ours once the distortion has been identified and removed. We are the ambassadors of the Creator who made it all. The real version of everything belongs to Him and therefore to us. There isn't anything the world can pull off that we can't take over and return to its rightful state. UpperDogs assume this. "The earth is His and everything in it."[29]

Everything is God's. Everything. Think about that simple statement for a moment. You wouldn't disagree. You would've said that yourself. And yet it's remarkable how differently we actually live. While we would say that everything belongs to God, we live as if nature belongs to him but everything else is the enemy's. But as we mentioned earlier, the enemy cannot create. Therefore every evil thing that man has ever come up with is a distortion—a distortion of something that God created, something inherently good. Evil things, ideas, and behaviors do exist of course, but only as perversions of a core godly nugget. They are a result of choices, not creation. So the same reality that applies to our "evil guy case subject" also applies to all the "stuff" of this world. To distort something is to do a secondary thing, not a primary one. The primary thing was done in the original creation. The distortion that the enemy accomplishes (and people in agreement with him) is always secondary to the original creative act of the Father. Let's look at any object—a gun for instance. It's made of metal. God's metal. The person who crafted it was given that crafting ability by God. This gun can be used for godly purposes or evil ones, as is true with any object. But no matter how it is used, it belongs to God.

In the *Splankna* book I shared this little parable:

> *One day a group of eminent scientists got together and decided that mankind had come a long way and no longer needed God. So they picked one scientist to go and tell Him that they were done with Him. The scientist walked up to God and said, "God, we've decided that we no longer need you. We're to the point that we can clone people and do many miraculous things, so why don't you just retire?" God listened very patiently to the man and then said, "Very well, but first, how about this: Let's have a*

Man-making contest." The scientist replied, "Okay, great!" But God added, "Now, we're going to do this just like I did back in the old days with Adam." The scientist said, "Sure, no problem" and bent down and grabbed himself a handful of dirt. God looked at him and said, "No, no, you go get your own dirt!"

-Author Unknown

UpperDog Christian walks with the clarity that all things around him belong to his team. Every evil thing made, had to use God's raw material. Evil is dependent on God. Isn't that a strange thought? Evil is dependent on God. There could not possibly be anything evil unless God created something in the first place, something that could be distorted. We walk through this world with a unique lens. Everything belongs to our team. The creator of it all is on our side. We have home court advantage.

What if we held to this UpperDog reality so clearly that any "new" thing proposed or experienced was assumed to have truth at its core no matter how obscured? It would make us so confident. We would be so hard to intimidate. We would be set free from our defensive guards around ideas, discoveries, developments, and released to really live like "it is good." Now just to be clear, we're not saying here that everything that appears evil is really good, or that everything evil can be turned into godliness. There is evil—but only as a distortion, only as rebellion. UpperDog Christian, armed with a redemptive theology, recognizes that no matter how far a particular evil campaign has developed its distortion, no matter how impressive the evil display, they had to start with God's "stuff," *because nothing else exists.*

The Love

Aaron is a messianic Jew who has every reason to deeply hate Arabs. But he doesn't anymore. When he came to Christ he was delivered of that hatred and given God's own love for Muslims. Upon crossing the border into Jerusalem one day, he was interrogated. When the guard didn't get the answers he was looking for, he took the opportunity to beat Aaron nearly to death. But then his life was changed.

Instead of retaliating, Aaron looked up from the cement, from the pool of blood in which he was lying and said, "I am sorry that I made you angry. I pray that you will forgive me. I know things are probably tough here in the West Bank for you and your family. I am going to pray to Jesus for you. I know that you hate me, but Jesus loves you and he said to love our enemies." He then leaned forward, and hugged the guard. The guard reported later that those words played over and over in his mind for days. "I could not forget those words," he said. "I realized that the people of my religion have plenty of weapons. We've had the best swords for 1,400 years now. We have plenty of hate that makes us want to kill anyone who gets in our way. But we don't have love. How could a Jew take that kind of beating from me and then turn around and show love to me? I had to find out. When a believer has the Word of God and the love of God in his heart, this is irresistible."[30]

If we really grab on to the full love of God for us, we will never be the same. One evening I was praying with Helen. I was asking God to show me his love for her. First, I saw a vision of Jesus separated from her and reaching for her. Then I felt something so powerful and overwhelming that I couldn't move. I felt energy in every cell of my body like an explosion. I felt the intense yearning of God. His love for Helen consumed me. It was so strong that I felt like I couldn't get close enough to her. It was truly unquenchable. I was amazed. The power of the Holy Spirit was so strong in me, that I was afraid to open my eyes or relax for fear that I would be overcome by it and explode. Yet it also felt incredibly wonderful to be so full of love. I tried to describe the love to her and I couldn't. There were no words. I asked, "God will you transfer this to her? Will you let her feel it?" When I prayed this, she squeezed my hands and began to cry. She felt his love for the first time.

Then she saw a vision in her mind's eye. She saw herself, where she had been a few months before, on her bathroom floor, crying and begging for death. But in that moment she saw it from God's perspective. There on the floor Jesus was wrapped around her like a blanket, holding her and comforting her. By the time we were done praying I had a whole new understanding of the immeasurable love of God—and so did she.

I realized in that moment that if we could truly understand, truly grasp and receive God's love, we would be complete. The love we receive in this world would feel like a bonus. God's love really does complete us. He fills all our needs with his love. Ever since that day, when I think of Jesus or hear the mention of his name, it makes my heart flutter. Like when I was a teenager and I met my husband. My heart would race, my skin would tingle, I felt a little bit giddy. Now I feel that way about Jesus. It sounds odd I know, but I actually yearn for him. I long to hear his voice. I get all excited when I have intimate moments with him.

There were eight of us sitting in a circle. We were strangers to one another. Our leader instructed us to complete this sentence: "I am _____." A heavy-set man with broad shoulders went first. "I am a man," he said. The gentleman to his left said, "I am an architect." I listened as they each took their turn. The woman next to me said with decided, intimate bravery, "I am uncomfortable with this exercise." The leader was impressed. My turn. What do I say? I am a lot of things, I thought to myself. I am a woman, a mother, a wife, a psychologist, a singer, an author…hmmm. I'm also all sorts of ugly things. I'm lazy. I'm prideful. I'm small and selfish, addicted and hypocritical.

"I am <u>a Christian</u>," I said.

(Leader not impressed.)

Ah, the noble answer. If there had been any other Christians in the group they would have been proud of me (and a little ashamed *they* didn't say that). But the unbelievers in that group were not roused. They didn't hear something that made them *want*. I didn't exactly draw all men unto him in that moment. They just noted me and looked to the next person. I wish I had responded differently. Why didn't I say, "I am? You're giving me a chance to state who I am? Fantastic! Here goes… 'I am <u>the object of the desperate, passionate love of the Creator of the universe who gave his life so he could be intimate with me</u>.'"

Now *that* they would've noticed.

That would've hit a touchstone in the people sitting in our little circle, even if they didn't let it show. Every one of them is centrally organized around the quest for love whether they know it or not. They want to love and they want to be loved more than anything else in the world. Everything they've ever done, from the shirt they chose in a department store, to their career direction, to their style of music is all grounded in the primal pursuit of love. We believe what we do because we think it's correct. And why is correct important? Because it makes us valuable, lovable. I choose what to wear, what to say, how to behave all based on what I believe is lovable. Although this is not entirely conscious to us, it remains our central organizing structure. Everything is about love,

And I know Him personally.

I have what they want. I'm the UpperDog. What would I be like as a person if that was truly my first, most obvious answer to the question? What if it wasn't rehearsed, wasn't manipulative, but was just what honestly gushes out of me? I'd be irresistible. People would have no choice but to ask, "What is with you?

Every October our little church dedicates an entire Sunday to hear an update of our works in missions. In this church of approximately 150 people, we support mission work in China, Uganda, Panama, and a Native American reservation in New Mexico. I've always been astounded by the amount of energy and resources that this slight quantity of people pour into missions. Every year without fail, we dedicate roughly $32,000 to missions alone. This number is separate from the money given for regular tithe, benevolence, and personal sponsorship of other Christian organizations. This made me curious. If our small church has such a huge impact, what does the rest of the world look like?

What I find most interesting is the unique love-machine of the Christian faith. We have a reward cycle built in. Our faith implores us take care of the orphans and widows. By being true to that call, by loving as God loves, our community of believers naturally grows. When I was a young child and was without food the church reached out. The church met our needs. As a natural aftereffect of that example, I have a desire to reach out, a heart for the hungry. The Bible says that we love because he first loved us. I call this the reward cycle. (I borrow that phrase from the *Love and Respect* book by Emerson Eggerichs[31].) The reward cycle of love in Christianity is a positive vicious cycle and it spins like this:

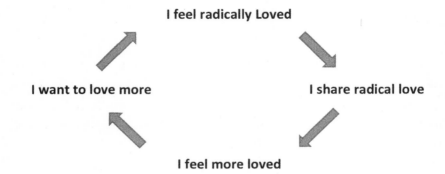

I feel radically Loved

I want to love more   **I share radical love**

I feel more loved

Once we start spinning on the reward cycle, we began to love more unconditionally, we obey more radically, and the world changes.

Every Christmas since I was a child, I've taken the opportunity to love back. This year for Christmas my family and I felt called to sacrifice part of our Christmas for a family in need. We wanted to provide food and gifts to a family who otherwise would have none. Remembering the impact this had on me as a small child, my hope was to impact others in the same way. Ever since that Christmas, I've known who meets my needs and I want to share that knowledge with others. What we see that the non-Christian misses is who it is that really provides our needs. Who really takes care of us!

On a selfish side, I also saw an opportunity to teach my children who (praise God) have never been in need. I specifically asked God to show us a family who was truly in need and a family that my kids could invest in. I wanted them to help shop, wrap, and deliver the packages. Maybe my kids will start the reward cycle by sharing radical love and realizing the love of Christ through the process. It doesn't matter where you begin, only *that* you begin.

After a few weeks of praying, God pointed us to the family we were to sponsor. Praise God we had an opportunity to be his hands and feet. My hope for this family was to recognize that God is taking care of them. God is their provider. My hope is that they recognize the real gift giver as God. My prayer is that they will begin to spin on the reward cycle.

See how Christianity is different? We really do have a unique reward cycle that occurs in our faith. No other faith loves like we do. We have thriving organizations that work on this unique dynamic. They reach out to the orphans and people in need. By "doing" love they are spreading the Word of Christ.

Compassion international was founded in 1952 because a Christian wanted to take care of Korean children who were impacted by the war. His desire was to take care of their essential need and share the love of Christ with them. By 2003, Compassion was helping and teaching 500,000 children. In 2013, ten years later that number grew to 1.5 million children.[32] World Vision started in 1950 by providing for the needs of children in America and quickly expanded to other countries. By 2003, World Vision with the help of millions of people was taking care of 2.2 million children. In the next ten years their number grew to 4.3 million children in almost 100 countries.[33]

In 1993 Samaritan's purse began a campaign called Operation Christmas Child. In the last 11 years 113 million shoeboxes have been delivered to children in approximately 150 countries. Through this work Samaritan's Purse has taken 2.8 million people through "The greatest Journey" a 12-lesson discipleship program.[34] These organizations thrive and grow because we are answering the call to be HIS hands and feet. We are taking the world—not by force—by love!

The Wisdom

"For the scientist who has lived by his faith in the power of
reason, the story ends like a bad dream. He has scaled the
mountain of ignorance; he is about to conquer the highest peak;
as he pulls himself over the final rock, he is greeted by a band
of theologians who have been sitting there for centuries."
—Robert Jastrow

Another area in which we have the upper hand is in science and philosophy. We represent the One who understands everything. We're forgetting that when we operate today as if the voice of "science" is stronger and somehow more legitimate.

Nicholas Copernicus was born in 1473. He was the first scientist to suggest that based on mathematics, the planets might actually revolve around the sun. Up until his time, it was assumed that the earth was the center around which everything else revolved. Copernicus was a believer. He was the earliest of a long succession of great, world-changing scientists who dove into the wild unknown in order to discover its intricacies. They did this *because* they believed in God. Sir Francis Bacon, Kepler, Galileo, Blaise Pascal, Isaac Newton and many others were the early fathers of science and all were motivated by deep faith in God. Even renowned philosopher Rene Descartes' famous injunction "I think, therefore I am" was only a precursor to his next assumption—his proof for the existence of God. He reasoned that only if God both exists and is reasonable and loving would it make sense for us to trust *our* reasoning abilities.[35] Sir Francis Bacon, known for developing the scientific method of inductive reasoning is quoted as saying:

It is true, that a little philosophy inclineth man's mind to atheism, but depth in philosophy bringeth men's minds about to religion; for while the mind of man looketh upon second causes scattered, it may sometimes rest in them, and go no further; but when it beholdeth the chain of them confederate, and linked together, it must needs fly to Providence and Deity.[36]

In other words, if you really stop and think about origins and the exquisite design of the universe, God is inescapable. These early revolutionary scientists believed that the universe was designed by an intelligent, loving, discoverable God who *wanted* to be known. They assumed that there was beauty and order to be found. Newton and Galileo were fond of saying that God gave us two books to read—the Scriptures and nature. They assumed that all investigation would only further confirm faith and a biblical worldview. And they were right. Even Albert Einstein, who never came to believe in a personal God, did concede that the universe had to be created intelligently. He said to a young pupil,

I want to know how God created this world, I am not interested in this or that phenomenon, in the spectrum of this or that element. I want to know His thoughts, the rest are details.[37]

But we're not here to argue for intelligent design. That's being done well in many other venues.[38] The point here is that Christians used to be highly respected *thinkers*. We used to lead scientific discovery and development. We used to be recognized as significant contributors to society. We used to operate in the scientific world with the upper hand. We used to know that our knowledge of the living God and creator gives us the edge on a confused world that's out of the loop. But slowly, somewhere along the way, we lost that edge. We have forgotten who we are, and the insider information we have at our disposal. We have allowed a tragic, unnecessary chasm to be formed between faith and thinking, faith and respectability. We've let go of our honored, valid position as ambassadors of the

King and of the Truth. But it's time to change that. It's time to remember who we are. We are the representatives of the one who *created* it all, who thought it all up.

At the end of the day, what we believe is either true or it's not.

If it's not, then "eat and drink for tomorrow we die."[39] But if it is true, then it is uncompromising. If it is true, then we have nothing to fear from scientific exploration. Investigation of what IS cannot possibly discredit the God who made it or those who follow him. If what we believe is true, then discovery will always prove us right. It has no choice. The scientific process is the slow, wondrous uncovering of his beauty and creativity. Every new unearthing screams, "Wow! God is gorgeous!"

Science and philosophy are tightly intertwined. Since science is limited to numbers, it is limited to matter and therefore has no direct relevance to studies such as theology or philosophy. But in order to make any sense of the numbers we have to have non-numerical propositions, ideas that are higher than numbers. So true science lies imbedded within philosophy. It depends upon it. Fr. Stanley L. Jaki makes the point that the "birth" of modern science, or the Scientific Revolution where we now apply quantities to investigation, was only possible because of the "fertile womb" that the Christian worldview provided.

He describes how science was "still birthed" in other cultures where Christianity was not the predominant foundation, but could not develop because their worldviews were insufficient to provide it's necessary philosophical underpinnings—namely that the universe we observe originated from a loving God with personhood who is separate from and above his creation, a God who not only created it, but perfectly ordered and orders it continually. This worldview assumes no conflict between reason and revelation. It was assumed that to discover more of nature was only to discover more of Him.[40]

Not only is there no opposition between science and faith, they are actually dependent on one another. Without a biblical worldview and the belief in an intelligent creator, science would be futile and well, unreasonable.

My husband and his friend Paul got revved up a few years ago. They felt called to start a discussion group at church open to anyone who wanted to bring difficult questions about Christianity to the table. They are both avid apologists at heart. They were ready to talk evolution, comparative religions, biblical historicity, cloning ethics, anything. One morning after church we were milling around in the lobby and my husband shared their idea with an acquaintance of ours. She listened, glassy-eyed for a while and then suddenly interjected, "Well I don't understand all that stuff. I just believe!" She said this as a point of pride, but I was embarrassed for her and for how commonly that attitude is displayed in Christendom. We act like "just believing" is higher than understanding, as if it's a deeper faith or submission. But I contend that the opposite is true. "Just believing" and forgoing understanding is lazy and irresponsible. Some Christians are too timid to ask the tough questions because at heart they are afraid that Christianity can't stand up to scrutiny. They are afraid that rigorous inquiry might disprove faith. Subsequently, we have not done our homework. We have not held on to the kind of disciplines that would have kept us respected as societal contributors.

We have become lazy thinkers.

Slowly and subtly the thinking disciplines have dropped by the wayside and our arguments have weakened, our minds have grown sluggish. We act like underdogs who assume that the world's thinkers have a leg up on us, like it's their house and not ours. We have bought their line that faith is archaic and irrelevant and contrary to rigorous philosophy. Or even worse, we secretly fear that investigation may destroy faith. We protect faith by closing off our minds, avoiding the philosophical and scientific platforms. But just as all scientific discovery has no choice but to make Christianity look good, philosophy is equally bound. Again, what we believe is either true or it's not. If it's true, then no honest philosophy can embarrass us. Jesus IS the Truth, after all, and we've been given his mind.[41] It's time to use it again. Our culture is thirsty for philosophical integrity, for an intellectual challenge. They're getting a twisted version of it from Deepak Chopra and Richard Dawkins while all along it is the Bride of Christ who's bearing the mysteries of the universe. Our position of "just believing" is not representing Jesus well in our culture. It is not respected. It is pitied, and rightly so.

Let's reclaim our upper hand in science and philosophy. Instead of fearing these disciplines, let's actively fund the advancement of science because we understand that its fruit can only shine a brighter light on our creator and we can't wait to see it happen yet again. Let's be the first to read up on the world's best philosophical attempts so that we can speak intelligently to the 21yr- old new age thinker at Starbucks. Let's make sure we know his worldview better than he does. Let's know it well enough to throw a wrench into it and earn a voice, a respected place at the table of thought. Let's be willing to put in the investment of time and effort required to be sharp thinkers. We have nothing to hide. We must return to being savvy philosophers, worthy debaters. We can afford it. The Holy Spirit promises to guide us into all truth. Let's take him up on it.

The Truth

"I know you hate me and you think I'm stupid." Every time my son was being disciplined he would come back with this statement. After about two weeks of missed opportunities, I confronted him. "Why do you keep saying that?" He froze and I saw that he was in deep thought. After a minute he conceded, "I don't know, I just keep hearing it," he explained. Instantly I recognized that it was a lie that was coming from warfare. I explained to him that he was hearing and believing a lie from the enemy. I asked him to pray and he repeated after me, "Lord God, I refuse the lie that mom and dad hate me and that they think I'm stupid. I accept the truth that they love me and that I am made in your image. I ask you to write all of the truth in my heart and heal it completely." He never repeated that lie again.

Christians may not have the line on perfect behavior but we do have the Truth. We have the Word of God, full of transformative truths.

We are dearly loved.	1John 3:1
We are his workmanship	Ephesians 2:10
We are fearfully and wonderfully made	Psalm 139:14
He is patient, not wanting anyone to perish	2 Peter 3:9
He will give you rest; take his yoke for he is gentle and patient.	Matthew 11:28-30
He provides all our needs.	Philippians 4:19
In Christ you are a new creation.	2 Corinthians 5:17
When we believe and repent we are cleansed of sin and guilt.	1 John 1:9 Acts 3:19

Those are just a few of the many truths of his character and his love for us. Neil Anderson's *Victory Over The Darkness*[42] has an exhaustive list of these pivotal truths. When you read the Bible and these many truths, put your name in those verses. See how much he cares for you.

But sometimes in order to embrace the truth we have to first recognize the lies we are believing. We cannot go around speaking these lies and letting them take root in our hearts. UpperDog trains his heart in the Truth. We know from Scripture that lies are the enemy's weapon. In John 8:44, Jesus describes Satan as "a liar and the father of lies." We know that the enemy comes to steal, kill and destroy."[43] One of his techniques is through these vicious lies. It starts out as a little whisper in our ear. Then that whisper takes root and we begin to embrace it. Once we buy into the lie, it becomes our reality.

Sometimes the lie can be very much like a truth. For instance, if I believe the lie that God won't let me get ahead financially. Maybe I've reasoned that he doesn't want to bless me, that the financial troubles are his way of protecting me from myself, or that I'm just not worthy. This must be true because every time I get a little extra cash, a bill for that very amount comes in too! See? God just won't let me get ahead.

On the flipside, what if I didn't buy into the lie? What if I believed the truth that God takes care of me? I may not have all the things I want, but I have what I need. Then I might see the same scenario very differently. I would make a different interpretation. Surprise sums of money that immediately go to an equivalent surprise bill would be seen as his kind provision instead of proof that he wants me destitute. Look! Every time an unexpected bill shows up, God has just finished giving us that very amount to cover it!

Lies play a huge role in how we approach life, relationships, our callings, etc. We need to examine our hearts. We need to ask God and our own hearts, "What are the lies I'm buying into?" We need to identify the lies, refuse them, and ask God to replace them with the truth. The truth is a significant part of being an UpperDog. We need God's truth. We need to understand it in every arena of life. In Isaiah 45:19, God says "I, the Lord, speak the truth; I declare what is right" We can seek the truth through the Word and we can seek the truth through the Spirit. Paul says, "We speak…in words taught by the Spirit, expressing spiritual truths."[44]

Even when we do know the truth, we are forgetful. It is in your nature and mine to forget. This is such a universal weakness in human nature that God commanded the Israelites to write the truth on their doorposts and on their foreheads![45] Take a minute now and ask God to show you the destructive lies that you've believed—that you still believe. As he shows you these lies, refuse them! Ask him to show you the truths you've forgotten, to write them in your heart and on your forehead. Through the Holy Spirit, we have the truth— let's embrace it! Let the truth win.

The Resources

Did you know that there are more Scriptures about money than there are about heaven and hell combined? God's big on money. He recognizes that exchange is fundamental to human life. It is central to societal navigation. It cannot be avoided. The early Christians who anticipated the immediate return of Jesus were quitting their jobs and pitching tents on the rooftops to keep a lookout. But they were re-directed. Paul instructed them to go back to work and continue the normal business of human exchange.[46] God knows money is in the middle of life. Finances are integral to everything. But he sees something about money that we don't see.

It is limitless and all of it is *his.*

Money is what's called "notional." It's only an idea, a representation. From our earthly perspective, down here in "The Matrix," money seems very real. So real that our predominant emotional reaction to it is worry. We worry because we are confused on two counts: we think money is both real and limited. Our entire financial paradigm is based on the belief that resources are fundamentally quantifiable. There is only so much of the good stuff around and I've got to make sure I get enough of it or the other guy will. But God disagrees. He acknowledges that we are stuck in the lack mentality but he's constantly calling us above it, inviting us to peek above cloud-line where there is no limit for our provider. He gives us wild imagery like "I own the cattle on a thousand hills."[47] And never once does he endorse our financial worries. There is never a time when he says, "Okay, now worry. It's time to be afraid. That really is the proper response right now." When it comes to money, we live in an alternate dimension. Our God has no limits on his resources. Financial worries are not only unnecessary for us, they are literally irrational.

In Mark 12 the religious leaders are trying to trap Jesus. They praise his character and then ask, "Is it right to pay taxes to Caesar?" Jesus says, "Show me a Denarius. Whose face is printed on it?" "Caesar's" they say. "Then give to Caesar what is Caesar's and to God what is God's" Jesus answers. One of the points here is that everything is God's, so "giving back to Caesar" doesn't matter.

Also in Mark 12, Jesus praises the widow who gave her last two coins to the temple treasury. The amount that the Pharisees gave was much greater but it was easy for them. What they gave did not threaten their comfortable lifestyle. But being a widow, this woman had no ongoing source of income. The beauty of the story is not only that she gave all that she had, but that she was displaying an act of fierce faith. Fierce, behavioral, put-it-all-on-the-line belief that she had a provider who would come through… that she could *afford* to be unreasonable.

In the spirit of that example, there have been several times when I was young and single and living on an unstable income when I gave to God more than was "reasonable" as an act of boldness, almost defiance. I have placed my last $50 in the collection plate to defy fear… to defy this world's illusion of lack. To say, "I *refuse* to embrace worry. I don't have to and I will not. I will put my money where my mouth is and my God will not let me starve for giving to him." "Bring the whole tithe into the storehouse!" he tells us in Malachi 3. "Test me in this! See if I will not throw open the floodgates of heaven and pour out so much blessing that you will not have enough room for it!

One time, several years back, I had an unusual vision. I guess you'd call it that. It was something like a train of thought that felt hijacked by the Holy Spirit. In my mind's eye I saw an unusual scenario. I imagined that I was driving and stopped at a red light. I heard a strange commotion outside and looked to my right to see a carjacker invade my front passenger seat. He quickly slammed the door and pointed his .45 squarely toward my chest. "Gimme the keys!" he commanded, visibly nervous and wired.

And then the strangest thing happened. Instead of throwing my hands in the air and complying in terror, I reached out and placed my hand on the gun. I felt compassion and peace rise within me and I smiled. "It's okay," I said gently. "You don't have to steal this car." His countenance changed from menacing to confused. "You can have it. It's a gift." He just stared at me, stunned. "You see, I belong to the God who owns everything. I can't be stolen from." He sat motionless as I reached for the keys and handed them to him. "This is a gift from God. Don't you dare go home and tell your family that you stole a car. You didn't. One was *given* to you by God."

How's that for a vision? Apparently, since I have yet to get the opportunity to play out this scenario in action, God was really trying to make a point here. He was giving me a vivid picture of what it would mean to really know who we are as children of the King who "owns the cattle on a thousand hills." The One who has no limit keeps a count of every hair on my head. He knows when every sparrow falls. He clothes the lilies of the field and the children of the Lord have never gone hungry.[48] When it comes to the financial side of life, we can afford to be at peace. We are financial UpperDogs. We are not promised great wealth in this life,

we are freed from it.

Because we are in him and he has all resources, we can afford to be peaceful in need, bold in request and outrageous in giving. We can learn "the secret" that Paul discovered in Philippians 4 of being truly content whether in plenty or poverty. We have the advantage that the world doesn't have: the knowledge that even in the worst case scenario, even if on this plane we literally starved to death, it would only culminate in the satisfaction of every need ever felt and then some. UpperDogs.

Have you seen *Les Miserables*?[49] If you haven't seen the movie or play, you definitely should. Valjean broke out of prison, and while on the run he came to a town and pursued shelter. The local minister fed him and gave him a place to sleep. Valjean, a desperate man, decides to rob the family. The minister awakes in the midst of the robbery and confronts him. Valjean hits him on the head and runs off. He doesn't venture far before the police arrest him. The police recognize that the loot in the bag belongs to the minister. They go to him and display the stolen silver to confirm that it belongs to him. To Valjean's amazement the minister, still nursing a head wound, informs the police that his items weren't stolen, but given as a gift. He then scolds Valjean for neglecting to take the silver candlesticks as well and he places them in the bag.

This minister is a serious UpperDog. He approached the situation as if everything belonged to the Lord, so he could afford to give Valjean a second chance. He warned him not to waste the opportunity he was given.

> *"The bishop approached him and said, in*
> *a low voice, 'Do not forget, ever,*
> *that you have promised me to use this silver to*
> *become an honest man.' Jean Valjean,*
> *who had no recollection of any such promise, stood*
> *dumbfounded. The bishop had stressed*
> *these words as he spoke them. He continued solemnly, 'Jean*
> *Valjean, my brother, you no longer belong to evil, but to*
> *good. It is your soul I am buying for you. I withdraw it*
> *from dark thoughts and from the spirit of perdition,*
> *and I give it to God!"*[50]

The minister's irrational response to the situation changed a thieving ex-convict. The transformation in Jean Valjean's character is glorious throughout the story. What if we lived like this minister? What if we truly embraced the idea that all resources belong to God? What if we were willing to radically follow the prompting of the Holy Spirit?

I (Heather) learned these lessons in a different fashion. I learned that all belongs to God by having very little. When I was young we were very poor. We went without most of the time. We didn't have any extras and we barely had the essentials. I remember one particular

Christmas when I was about 13. My mom had cancer and my stepdad was laid off for the winter. Because he worked for a small family-owned business we didn't get the luxury of unemployment. We had no income. Our cupboards were bare and there were no gifts under the tree. But when all seemed lost, God provided. A church in our little town knew of our situation. They provided food and a gift for each of the five children. There are many examples in my life when only by the supernatural power of God we had our needs met.

My desperate need opened my eyes to the generosity of God. I could have become embittered that I had so much less than everyone else. Instead, I learned was that God is my provider. As an adult my husband and I work hard to achieve financial peace. We know that all we have belongs to God and we want to be good stewards of his resources.

I remember a conversation I had with God when I was new in private practice and I was deciding how much to charge my clients. I was basically trying to convince God that I shouldn't charge as much as I felt he was leading me to. He reminded me of my conviction that all that I have belongs to him. He said, "All that *they* have belongs to me too, you know." I hadn't thought of that. I was holding a double standard in conviction. It's either all his or it's not! From that moment on, I charged what God said to charge and if I ever felt a desire to give a discount, I asked the Holy Spirit. I realized I should never assume that I know what his plans are. My understanding is limited and his is endless, just like his resources. Consider this story:

A poor woman called a local radio station asking for assistance with groceries. She said she had faith that God would provide. A Satanist overheard the broadcast and decided to shame the woman. He got her address, called his secretary and ordered for food to be taken to her. "And when she asks who sent her the food," he ordered wryly, "tell her it's from the devil." The woman was so happy receiving the food. The secretary then asked, "Don't you want to know who sent you the food?" The woman answered, "No my dear, it doesn't matter. When God orders, even the devil obeys!"

The Comfort

Christian or not, this life can be hard. Horrible and unmentionable things happen to us just like everyone else. The problem arises when we embrace the similarities but not the differences. Like the world, we live as if today's trials are our undoing. I know this all to well; I've been there.

By the time I (Heather) started high school, I had suffered abuse of many forms and great loss. My mom had been dealing with cancer and my step-dad's job was unstable. Not ideal circumstances for a family of seven. Even though I was young I had already been earning money for a couple of years. I de-tasseled corn, babysat and worked for a neighbor doing odd jobs and gardening. I took care of my own essential needs and helped out where I could.

My freshman year in high school I met a senior who was the *perfect* guy. He was patient with my youth and innocence and he didn't expect me to do the things the older girls did. He seemed to genuinely care for me and want to protect me. I felt safe with him. He was in the military, which took him away for training and deployment a couple of times during our relationship. We had our ups and downs like every teenage couple, but I was pretty confident that he was my gift from God. Never before had I ever felt so safe and taken care of. Never before had I been the center of someone's universe. He didn't care about my past of abuse; he just wanted a future with me. For the first time, I could picture a promising life ahead.

But then my world stopped. The second day of my junior year I arrived home to the news, "Robert was in a head-on collision with a semi on the bridge. He didn't make it."

No more hope. No more future. Everything I had gone through, all of the abuse and loss of other loved ones, nothing broke me like that moment. That was the day I stopped breathing. The day I stopped believing in hope.

Everyone experiences moments like these...
"You have cancer."
"You're fired."
"I want a divorce."
"She has two months to live."
"We regret to inform you..."

Such moments seem so monumental that "future" becomes an incomprehensible word. There is no tomorrow, only today. No one would deny the devastation of these traumas. When people try to reassure us, it lands on deaf ears. We are paralyzed by the severity of the moment and nothing makes sense like it used to. It's almost like we go into a spiritual shock. All of our foundations are shaken like an earthquake and we are shattered.

These are natural human responses to living in a fallen world where terrible things happen. As Christians, we believe that God will work this out to our good, that he has a plan for us. We just don't know how. The fact is that these things are going to happen. Trouble falls on the righteous and the unrighteous. We are going to lose focus.

But "we don't mourn like those who have no hope."[51] The truth is that we do have a hope and a comfort that can sustain us. We have the hope of reuniting with those we love. We know that God is working in our lives and that he is holding our hearts. We have a God who walked in this world, a God who humbled himself to suffer in ways similar to us. He knows what it's like to suffer loss.

We have a God who empathizes with us. Jesus has been there himself and he is here for us now. It's unrealistic to believe that we need to be strong enough to never be shaken. We will be shaken. God is the one who is strong enough. When our foundation moves he is always the same. He is our strength. Scripture does not say that he won't give us more than we can handle. It says that when (not if) we are weak, HE is our strength. He has all the resources we need to go through any trial in this world. With blurry eyes and broken hearts, we need to gaze upon our maker. He is the only one who can get us through.

We also need to remember that we don't have to *stay* in pain and despair. Even though we go through the same traumas and feel similar emotions as the world, we need not lose hope. Hold on to hope—it's worth the fight. Remember who holds your tomorrow. When storm clouds roll, don't act like you've never seen the sun. Remember that you've been in that place before and you survived; you smiled again, you laughed again. And not only can you survive, you can thrive. You can let God strengthen you. You can let God teach you. You can stop blaming him and trust that he will turn the ashes into beauty. Remember that he suffered when he didn't need to. I'm not just talking about the cross. He suffered the pain of living in this fallen world. Let that be your comfort. He does know what you are going through.

Let's do a little guided imagery. Imagine Jesus as your personal trainer staring into your eyes, not blinking and not looking away. He is walking backward in front of you, never losing eye contact. He assures you, "You can do this. I will help you. Just follow me. I've got you. You can trust me. I love you enough to die for you. I know all and I see all. You need only follow me." Imagine yourself with your eyes locked on him. Everything else seems hazy as you stare back into his eyes. You don't need to look past him or to your left or right. You don't need to look at the ground below. He knows where your every step will land. He knows every obstacle in your way. As long as you focus on him, you will not stumble, you will not get lost. Just keep your eyes on him.

When you imagine this scene, can you see the love in his eyes? Can you see the yearning of the one who cares for you in a way you've never known in this lifetime? If not, do it again. We are never a burden to him. We are the love of his life. In return, he is the very air we breathe. When you are struggling, take a deep breath and remember.

The Hope

I (Sarah) have never known what it's like to be an unbeliever. I was raised in faith. I literally cannot imagine what it would feel like to have no hope, to walk through a day thinking that everything ends in my meaningless, eventual disappearance. The perception that everything is just dust returning to dust is the ultimate nihilism. I look at unbelievers and think, "How on earth do they get up in the morning?" Hopelessness saturates secular philosophy. It is the constant quiet rumble beneath every fallen effort and vain accomplishment. The world is all too familiar with the fruit of hopelessness. Remarkably, nearly 38,000 Americans take their own lives every year. Suicide is the 3rd leading cause of death among young people ages 15-24 and the 10th leading cause of death overall.[52] Why? There are many reasons of course, but simple hopelessness is a major theme. No matter the level of current success, health, financial security or fame, without the Gospel and the promise of eternity, it all comes to nothing. The closest the unbeliever can come to hope is some vague idea of "making a difference" for future generations… a difference they will never get to enjoy. The futility is staggering.

In swoops UpperDog with the only legitimate hope in the universe… Jesus.

Jesus infuses every moment with hope and meaning. He gives everything a reason. Literally every human being you will ever encounter is desperate for hope and you have it to give. You don't just have *some* hope, you have the *only* hope. The biblical reality is the only offering of hope in human history. Now that's real leverage.

Nobody wonders if they need hope. No rebellious sinner or hardened atheist has trouble relating to hopelessness. It doesn't require scriptural adherence for its validation. Hopelessness is pandemic and you carry its cure.

I love the show "Shark Tank." Ambitious entrepreneurs pitch their products and ideas before a small panel of "sharks," millionaire business moguls who are there to consider investing. When the sharks see something they like, they'll even squabble over who can make the best offer and secure a new promising investment angle. But when they see little potential in the pitch, they share their feedback with the disappointed guest. One of the most common reasons they decline on investing is because they feel like the market to which the new product applies is too narrow. "It's too much of a niche product." Well, that criticism could never be aimed at Christianity. Literally every person who has ever lived needs the hope of the Gospel. UpperDog knows it. [wag]

The Joy

It's my favorite verse: "For the joy set before him, Jesus endured the cross and its shame."[53]

For the JOY.

Isn't that surprising? Wouldn't you think it would be for the LOVE? Or maybe for the OBEDIENCE that he submitted to the cross? But no. Scripture states that the core thing that motivated Jesus to yield to the cross was the JOY set before him. What was that joy exactly? And how was it "set before him?" The joy set before him was all that he could see coming. It was all that he knew the cross was going to accomplish:

The final payment for all sin,
   The total defeat of the enemy, sin and death,
      The reconciliation of mankind to the Father,
         The repair of creation,
            The restoration of man's authority to reign with Him,
            The wedding feast of the Lamb!

Christians! That's a whole lot of JOY! This is a great story we're in! The centerpiece of the gospel is joy! Not sin, or conviction or the fear of hell, or righteousness or service, or Scripture or even worship, but JOY! The center of the story is joy. I think that without realizing it, we've lived as if the Gospel is righteousness-based. The point of being a Christian is being good. But that is not what Jesus says. He says that all these things are serving the joy and flowing from it. It was joy that caused him to lay his wrists against that wood. Everything is "for the joy."

"I met angels!," she said with excitement. Cynthia came to see me because of depression and a sense of disconnection from God. He met her through our work and cleared out several blocks in her heart. Subsequently, she began to move in her gifting for the first time. As a child she had had several experiences with seeing into the heavenly realms, but that seemed to be over, until now. In that twilight time when she wasn't quite asleep but wasn't quite awake, she was suddenly aware of angels around her. As she recounted the story to me I celebrated with her. "What were they like?" I asked. "They were happy!" she said. "Happy?" "Yes! They were smiling and laughing and joking with each other."

Playful angels? I was surprised. I didn't realize it until that moment, but I think I expected angels to be serious. I imaged them strict, dutiful, intense and sober. I thought they'd be in battle mode, engaged in the great heavenly war. I imagined them all still in Daniel mode. Remember the Daniel account? The angel shows up in response to Daniel's petition panting and harried. He apologizes for taking three weeks and explains that he was detained by the Prince of Persia. He had to battle his way through to Daniel and now he'd have to battle his way back out with Michael's help.[54] Serious.

But the war is no longer raging. The victory has been won for over two thousand years and the party is already underway. The angels testify. Since then I have heard many more similar accounts of the joyful state of the angel hosts by those who get to peek behind the veil. Of course there are still warrior angels, I'm sure. There are still serious moments and tasks. But overall the heavens are in joy.

Remember how we're the ones with hope and a future? Well joy and hope are intimately connected. Outside of the Gospel, outside of a secure future, there can be no true joy. There can only be a temporary tease. Without the Gospel and the promised hope of eternity, every quasi-joy experienced here has an expiration date. It is tainted by entropy, doomed to end. Think about the greatest joys for the unbeliever. Maybe having babies, experiencing deep beauty, loving and being loved? Without the Gospel, these things are excruciatingly temporary. Only the Christian has the assurance that every hint, every taste of joy on this plane is a whisper of the fullness to come. Only UpperDog has access to true joy. In this very moment, all of heaven is partying. There is a huge smile painted across the cosmos. UpperDog can't help but grin just thinking about it.

The Authority

Ah, the big bad government. Surely we're the underdogs politically. I mean come on, look at the state of the state! We have open homosexuality in the military, legalized abortion, prayer banned in schools, an executive branch enacting things like the right to use force against the American public. Things are looking grim.

But we get a different perspective in 2 Samuel 1 and in Romans 13 where we're told that all government leaders are established by the Lord. If we understand that the leaders over us, no matter what their leanings, are appointed by the Lord, we never need to see ourselves as victimized by government. We can enter into partnership with the Lord's purposes through a particular leader. What is God up to in our country? What good is he working in the big story through this mayor, governor, or president?

Remember my client who was always worrying about the government? I explained this to her. I exposed that when she concentrates so much on the government, it becomes a thief that steals her vitality and her attention. We all have to recognize our own weaknesses. Her weakness is to be overcome and anxious due to political issues. I gave her homework to stop listening to talk radio, stop feeding this negative giant that was growing inside. Don't get me wrong; I think it's important to be informed. However, some are vulnerable to paranoia and unnecessary anxiety. Government is her kryptonite. She did her homework and took a break. She listened to worship music and began to feel peace. She began to return to her root belief that God was in control. She fed her faith instead of her fears. The government giant lost its power over her. She learned about her limitations and now she can stay informed without being overwhelmed. If she feels like it's starting to get the best of her, she takes it to God. She puts it in his hands and gets it off of her mind. She doesn't feed the giant.

How much control does government really have over issues of faith? Consider this… can anyone ban prayer? How can they stop us? Isn't prayer personal? We can pray anytime, anywhere we want. We don't need others to hear it for it to be effective. We don't need someone to give us permission. God can hear our thoughts; we have an open line of communication that no one can stop. What a profound gift prayer is, and God created it in such a way that no one can take it away. No individual, no group and no government.

And then there's my friend Arlene. She discovered (the hard way) who really has the authority in this life. Arlene's parents died within two weeks of each other; her mom was only 52 years old. She was devastated and overwhelmed with anguish and responsibility. She had three children and nowhere to turn. A neighbor offered "Just what she needed." Arlene's life took a dramatic turn that day. A life of drug addiction began. She required funds to support her addiction. She stole without conscience, even from her twin sister. She began dealing drugs as well. She was one of the 50 most wanted criminals. With her name in the newspapers and her face on television, eventually this life caught up with her. She was arrested, facing 36 felony charges and 6-12 years in prison.

She was shattered the day she went to court regarding her children. The judge was exasperated. He saw a wretched pitiful excuse of a mother before him. He saw a woman who would rather feed her addiction then take care of her children. Arlene begged him, "Please don't take away my children, I love them!" The disgruntled judge looked at her with loathing in his eyes and stated that she should have been thinking about her children when she was out committing crimes and doing drugs. Repulsed, he told the officers; "Get her out of my courtroom." The lawyer informed her that if she were given six or more years, the result would be automatic loss of parental rights. She wouldn't even be able to know where they were. Remember, she is facing 6-12 years. This would be justice! This is what Arlene deserved and even she wouldn't argue.

Arlene was given an 11-year prison sentence. All hope was lost and she wanted to die. This is when she finally gave in to the countless invitations from her fellow inmates to go to church. This is when she began to hear the message of the gospel—Jesus is your rescuer; he can take away your sin and your pain. She fell to her knees and with a sincere heart she gave her sin, her life and her heart to Jesus.

Everything began to change. Arlene sought God with all her heart, soul, mind and strength. The social worker on her case had personally devoted herself to making sure Arlene never saw her kids again. She told Arlene she didn't deserve her children and they were better off without her. Arlene acknowledged that in her current state she was not worthy of her children and they deserved better. However, she knew God was changing her and she told the social worker, "Wait and see. God is doing a mighty work in me and through him I will be the mom they need and deserve." She knew now who really controlled her fate—not the social worker or even the judge—Jesus was in control. Arlene began to embrace her UpperDog position.

The next time she stood before this judge, she was a very different woman. She walked into that courtroom knowing that God had the upper hand. The judge was astonished at the change he saw in her. He told her that he had never seen so much beauty come out of such horridness. He commended her for the changes she'd made. Arlene regained custody of her children. She learned the valuable lesson of being completely reliant on God. She knew then and she knows now that God is the one who holds her future. When you think all is lost because of the authorities in your life, remember who your true authority is!

You know, it's a very rare individual who *means* to be evil. Only the rare human caricature wakes up in the morning, twists his mustache and asks, "What terrible mischief can I stir up today?" For the most part, our government leaders are not intending to do evil. They are doing what they think is right. I know it's frustrating. Some of the things they do are clearly wrong, but they don't always see it. Most of them really believe that what they are doing is right. So what then shall we do? We *pray* for them. We pray that God will reveal what is right. That *he* will show them. That *he* will lead them.

The Life

Just about the worst Christian scenario anyone can come up with is martyrdom. That's the big, dark threat. What if God called me to be killed for my faith? Well, he could. People have died for faith throughout human history. Jesus assured us that, "If they persecuted me, they will surely persecute you."[55]

We'll call him Jamal. He's a Christian leader in the Middle East. "You have to be a little bit crazy to serve Christ in the Middle East," he says with a smile. "I think every Christian should go to jail at least once for his faith in Christ. After that, the only thing left for them to do to us is kill us. But that is the best blessing of all. Once they kill us, we are with Jesus forever!"[56]

In the classic *Foxe's Book of Martyrs* we read, "The history of Christian martyrdom is, in fact, the history of Christianity itself; for it is in the arena, at the stake, and in the dungeon that the religion of Christ has won its most glorious triumphs. We witness a soul so under the influence of God, that evil, even in its most cruel form, cannot dim its beauty, but serves as a constant to heighten its luster.[57]

When my youngest child was a little over a year old, I started to worry about him. He seemed to be sick often. One night it occurred to me that I could lose him. As I began to think about that, my heart went in a surprising direction. I had this huge realization that if I lost him today, I couldn't complain. A year and half with him was more than enough of a blessing. Maybe because I was infinitely aware that he was an unexpected gift from God. Or maybe because my love for God grew every day as I was reminded of his blessings through this little guy. Either way, I was surprised at my own heart reaction. I really *did* feel that way. I genuinely felt such a thankfulness that I knew even if God took him back, my blessing was greater than the loss. I had already enjoyed 18 months of this miraculous gift. Of course, I didn't want to give him back, and I'm tremendously thankful that wasn't God's plan, but if it had been, I could still be thankful.

Remember I told you the story of how I lost a boyfriend when I was 16. I felt the exact opposite in the face of that teenage trauma. I remember hearing, "It's better to have loved and lost, then never to have loved at all," and I thought that was the biggest lie I had ever heard. I was determined that there was no way that I was actually better off just because I had loved him. Love only brought pain. It was *not* worth it.

Why do I see such an amazing contradiction between the loss of my boyfriend and the potential loss of my son? When I was younger I had a very narrow understanding of eternity. Over the years God has taught me so much about how small this life is. Francis Chan illustrated this best. One night while speaking, he stretched out a long rope in front of the audience. He explained that the rope represents our existence in time. He then pointed to one end of the rope where there was about a two inch space wrapped in red tape. "This is your life on this earth," he said.

That is why we don't need to mourn like those who have no hope. We do have hope. We have eternity. We have forever. If we lose someone in this life, it's just a "day" that we are without him or her. If only we could get in touch with the thankfulness of the days we did get to spend with those people. Let's listen to the advice of our Father who understands this in a way we cannot. He reminds us that we are to think about whatever is lovely. Grief over loss is legitimate and important but it is not meant to be permanent. I really believe that we choose our misery. Sometimes, all we need to do is take off the goggles that keep our vision narrow and look around. Earlier in the book we talked about how even in the most evil person there is still more of God's glory than evil. I believe that is also true in our darkest hour. There is still so much more beauty, love, comfort, and relationship. It's like we look so intently at the pain that we miss all the rest. I imagine God is in our peripheral vision imploring us to look around, open our eyes and see the beauty even *in* the ashes.

The Power

One of our Splankna Practitioners tells this story:

"Our small missions team had only two weeks in Rwanda to visit with our friends from our sister church in Byumba. The first evening we

traveled to that remote village, met our gracious hosts and slept under mosquito netting. The next morning, seated on rough-cut logs in their open-air church, we watched as people from the surrounding villages gathered to worship. After the service, a woman approached me in broken English and asked if I would please pray for her friend. Two women walked another woman over to me. She had deep yearning in her eyes. Because I didn't know what she needed, I prayed in my prayer language, speaking in tongues, a form of praying which gave me confidence I would be praying the will of God for her. After praying just a few minutes all four women threw their hands up in the air and began to squeal with excitement. They waved their hands and danced around. I didn't know what was happening. 'What did I say?' I asked. 'You don't know?' she exclaimed. No, I didn't know what I had said.

She told me that I had just prayed in the Kinyarwanda language and that I had spoken the highest blessing that a Kenyan Rwandan woman could possibly dream of. I had spoken a blessing in their language that said the woman would have many, many cows. In their culture, cows represent all of one's possessions. God had spoken through me, not only in their language, but in their specific cultural idiom! I stood in awe."

How fun is that! The Holy Spirit is alive and active now, this very moment. Thousands of Christians, post first century, have experienced the power of God moving through them. Many are well known now, like John G. Lake, Agnes Sanford and Heidi Baker. But countless more, everyday Christians like you and me can tell you stories that would make you hunger. They would make you hope. Phil Mason tells the colorful story of praying for a woman with a chunk of glass lodged in her foot. As they prayed for her healing, in the middle of a busy conference, the chard of glass literally appeared on the floor beside her foot. At Bethel Church in Redding California they have seen many tumors disappear and limbs regenerate. They have watched blind eyes restored to sight. The famous Azusa St.

revival in 1906 saw miracles of many forms. Eric Metaxas recounts many current-day miracle stories in his book, *Miracles: What They Are, Why They Happen, And How They Can Change Your Life.*[58]

At our last Master's Training for Splankna, we had our own little encounter. During a teaching on some heavy emotional content, one of our attendees became tearful and upset. Heather and I laid hands on her and we all prayed together for the Lord to calm her heart. As she was praying, Heather felt prompted to ask that Jesus might send us an angel army to attend to us. The moment she spoke the words, the roof of our building rumbled suddenly and loudly, as if a thousand feet landed on it all at once. Everyone smiled and laughed and thanked God. It may not make the evening news, but the attendance of angels, transcendence in worship, encounters with the Lord himself, and the miraculous power of the Holy Spirit are all alive and well and living in your neighborhood. Whether or not we're well-skilled in availing ourselves of it, UpperDog Christian is especially connected to the power source of all things.

The Victory

"Islam is cracking from the inside," reports Hamdi, a former Palestinian guard. Jesus is reaching out to the people of the Middle East and they are responding in record numbers. Muslims who have never come in contact with a Christian are experiencing Jesus himself. He is literally appearing to them and saying, "Reject Allah. Come to me." And they are. Millions have given their lives to Christ in the last ten years.[59]

Kareem was born into a Catholic Palestinian family in Bethlehem but he had rejected faith completely. He became an angry atheist, bitter at the "joke" of the endless lines of pilgrims kissing the spot where Jesus is said to have been born at the Church of the Nativity.

He attended a Christian service one day "to laugh at the poor, helpless people who are so deceived." But he would be surprised.

He tells the story this way: "The pastor stood at the front of the church. I looked down the aisle and saw a man in a white robe standing next to him. He was looking straight at me. I asked my friend sitting next to me who that man was standing next to the pastor. 'I don't see anyone standing next to the pastor,' my friend replied. 'He's alone up there.' But he wasn't alone. The man next to him was wearing a white robe, and his eyes appeared to be looking right through me. He said, 'I love you, Kareem. Come to me.' All I know is that when he spoke to me and his eyes met mine something overwhelmed my heart so strongly that I got out of my chair and ran down the aisle, sobbing like a baby. I couldn't resist him."[60] Stories like these abound all around the world. Jesus is on the move.

This year on Mission Sunday (that's what we call it) a group who is specifically dedicated to the work in China gave a presentation. They asked our congregation a question: "Of the four major religions in the world—Hinduism, Buddhism, Islam, and Christianity—which one is growing the fastest?" Despite popular misconception that Islam is taking over, the answer is actually Christianity. By the middle of this century, if the current growth rates stays the same, there will be three billion Christians in the world—one and a half times the number of Muslims.[61]

In 1900, there were approximately 10 million Christians in Africa. By 2000, there were 360 million. By 2025, conservative estimates see that number rising to 633 million. Those same estimates put the number of Christians in Latin America in 2025 at 640 million and in Asia at 460 million.[62]

Despite the misconceptions, the Gospel is prevailing. Christianity is taking over. This reality of Christianity's explosive growth is one of the great-untold stories of our time—a story that North American Christians need to hear.[63] Throughout all human history, Yahweh reigns. No civilization, no government, no false religion or creed has ever been able to stamp out the fire of Christianity. The most violent persecution has only stoked the flame. Criticism has only sparked renewal. Neither death nor life, angels nor demons, the present or the future, not height or depth or anything else in all creation will ever be able to separate us from the Love of God in Christ Jesus.[64]

We are winning.
We always have been, and we always will.
Until ALL things are placed under his feet.

Ambassadors in Action

So what? So we have the remarkable advantage. We're on the winning team. We cannot be conquered, stolen from, humiliated or killed. How does that change a Tuesday morning?

Most Christians have read a stack of books on good moral behavior. We're familiar with discussions about responding in grace and love instead of road rage and egotism. These are wonderful books and important lessons. We always strive to represent love in the world. That's the established starting place. Thankfully, I feel like that ground is being well covered in modern Christian writing and media. But WWJD covers more than "Be good." The Gospel is a complete worldview, and worldview colors everything.

On The Offense

So here we want to look at our ambassadorship through another lens. We want to look at how our inherent advantage allows us to live and move in culture, not only from the posture of Christ-like gentleness and grace, but also from a proactive posture. Christianity on the Offense. I don't mean "offensive" (although sometimes that's required). I mean on the offense as opposed to the defense. Christianity that acts on the world instead of merely *reacting* to it. Because we have the advantage, we are afforded the offense. Our position in Christ does not just give us freedom from the brokenness of the world, but the power to change it. We are meant to be active players. Movers and shakers. Culture shifters. The upper hand means we're the ones at the cultural helm. I realize that it doesn't look that way, but that's only because we haven't gotten a good grip.

Jesus tells us that it is their gates that shall not prevail against us[65]. I want you to notice something about that statement. He says that their "gates" shall not prevail. Gates are defensive. A gate is what you build to protect yourself against someone stronger. You hide inside your gate to stay safe. Jesus is unapologetically placing the enemy's camp in the defensive position. He's saying that it's the lie that is in the weak position, not the truth. It's the secular culture that's in danger. They've set up their gates and still they won't prevail against those with the advantage. We're on the offense and we will prevail. UpperDog lives on the offense. He holds a worldview that assumes he fundamentally acts on his environment rather than being acted upon. He sees all situations through the lens of potential.

Last week I got an email from a witch. (Ah, if I only had a dime for every time I've started a paragraph that way.) She had come across our website and was offended by our statement that witchcraft is "the pursuit of special knowledge or power outside of God."[66] She wrote a lengthy email about how I clearly misunderstand not only witchcraft but Jesus as well. "If you really knew about Jesus," she explained, "you would know that he was one of the most important pagans of all time." Wow.

The underdog in me would've gone into defensiveness and fear. Defensive for my position both on witchcraft and on Jesus, and fear that I was dealing with a witch! I could have quickly erased the email and prayed for spiritual protection over myself and Splankna and stopped there, hoping she didn't infect me with her contact.

But the UpperDog in me knows better. "Hello Alana," I began. "I really appreciate your thoughtful comments. You are obviously very studious and serious about your worldview. I respect a deep thinker. I'm really glad you contacted me." From there I went on to explain the differences between her worldview and mine, particularly on the issue of Jesus and who he is. I received her, legitimized what I could in her, and gained a voice.

The advantages we've outlined are what *afforded* me this kind of response. I can afford to validate a witch. Why? Because I really do hold the truth. There's no need for fear or defensiveness when I'm already the winner. There's no reason to berate her either. Berating her would only come from an over-compensation in me—a place that isn't quite sure I really know the truth and therefore has to resort to a power struggle. The only people Jesus berated were the religious leaders. This woman desperately needs what I have to give. She's the one in the weak position. My advantage allows me generosity and generosity earns me a voice. UpperDog's advantage allows him to genuinely love the sinner while rejecting the sin.

The offense applies to every arena of life: relationships, politics, health, education, finances, everything. Relationally we're afforded generosity and humility, intimacy and honesty, because no rejection is our definition, no loss our end. Politically we know that leaders are God-appointed and so we vote decisively and speak boldly. We can afford, like Martin Luther King, to stand up for God's design in strength and boldness because no gunshot can beat us. No sly academic argument can overwhelm us and so we can engage the table of ideas with eloquence. We can give irrationally where there is no clean water, and take on needs that are beyond us because our finances are unlimited. The more deeply we can dig our toes into the warm sand of the Christian reality, the taller we will stand.

Troublemakers

Part of Christianity on the offense is actually offensive. We are meant to cause trouble. Have you ever thought about what a pain in the neck Jesus was for his culture? (Yes, I put that in print). He caused many more riots than sing-alongs. Among our family of Splankna practitioners, one of the phrases I'm famous for is, "You can't do anything of consequence without ticking somebody off." And it's true. If the secular world around you is perfectly pleased with you, you're laying low.

The biblical edict of "speaking the truth in love" is the perfect summary to our ambassadorship discussion.[67] "The truth in love," is the perfect description of the rejection of both passivity and aggression in our cultural stance. To speak the truth is to move away from passivity. To do it in love is to move away from aggression. No extremes, no over-compensation, just the truth in love. That is what Jesus did. He went around speaking. He said what no one else would say. He told the truth without fail and we can be sure that he always did it in love because he was Love in the flesh. And even in that behavior, that perfect ambassadorship of the Father in his culture, he was the most famous troublemaker of all history. They killed him for it. And not just because it was the pre-ordained will of the Father. They *wanted* to kill him. He was offensive.

But here's the kicker.

He could *afford* to be.

He could afford to be offensive because he knew he had already won. He could afford to speak and act the truth no matter the cost because he knew his advantage. He knew the position he held. He knew that if they reviled him, he could retreat and rest in his Father's validation. If they stole from him he could pull a coin from the mouth of a fish. If they disagreed with him, his truth would prevail. If they beat him, his blood would testify to the nations. And if they killed him—when they killed him—in that would be the greatest victory of all.

Jesus could afford anything, and so he went for it, head held high and voice raised. He loved lavishly, convicted piercingly and moved powerfully, because no one had anything on him. And then when it was finished, he placed you and me in his own seat. We were placed in him at the right hand of the Father. He made you the UpperDog with him. He could afford anything. And so can you.

Be the one who challenges educational policy at your child's school. Be the one who calls out sin in yourself, your relationships, your church. Be the one who shows up at downtown soup kitchens and political rallies. Be the one who starts the "pay it forward" line at Starbucks. You know, where you secretly pay for the person's order in line behind you? Hug the person who everyone avoids. Give speeches. Write books. Disagree with the popular opinion. When you see a need, spend like you grow it. Love lavishly, convict piercingly and move powerfully.

You can afford it.

Section 3

Theological Underdogs

Now we're shifting gears a bit. Let's look at how we deal with God himself. Once again, the lens of passivity and aggression is useful in describing the theological underdog. Both imbalances inhibit our productive partnership with Jesus. First we'll look at how we can be passive with God and with warfare. Then we'll explore what it looks like to be aggressive both with God and warfare.

(And after that, the best part is last.)

Theological Passivity

"God is more anxious to answer than we are to ask."
—Smith Wigglesworth

Pawns On A Chessboard

When we lose touch with our UpperDog status, we can take on those same imbalances of ungodly passivity and aggression not only in our dealings with culture, but also in our lives with God. We can lose sight not just of our ambassadorship in the world, but of our partnership with him. First we'll explore how passive theology plays out.

To put it most simply, passive theology says that we have no part in this story at all. Our faith has no bearing on what does or doesn't happen in this life. This Calvinistic abuse purports that because God is sovereign, we have no significant input whatsoever. This is the imbalanced position that I (Sarah) was covertly taught growing up. No one would've said out loud that we are insignificant in the big story. There was just the absence of any theology of contribution outside of direct evangelism. Our only part, this theology would explain, is to walk in holiness and convert new believers (both true and crucially important). But that's where our part ends. The sovereign Lord runs it all and I'm just an observer, waiting for the next chapter to begin when all things are made new.

Underdog Christianity likes to quote that, "the prayer of a righteous man is powerful and effective," but would never dream of stopping the rain like Elijah did, even though that's the very next passage. James assures us that Elijah was "a man, just like us"[68] when he stopped the rain and when he started it again, but this is the side of Christianity that believes the "miraculous" ended with the apostles and the Holy Spirit no longer moves in power through believers. This position is exemplified in C.S. Lewis's famous quote, "I don't pray to change God. I pray to change me." We love ya' Clive, but that statement is hogwash. A statement like that implies that the only purpose for prayer is personal development in holiness—that prayer is not really meant to bring anything about *outside* of me. Prayer is relegated to a discipline for discipline's sake. But Elijah didn't pray to change himself. He didn't pray to become more holy.

He prayed to stop the rain.

Let's admit that. And Scripture's reference of it assumes we will do the same. After all, he "was a man just like us." Passive theology sees personal holiness as the chief aim of Christianity. The passive Christian is well aware of the great commission and the ever-present call to evangelize, but outside of that he misses partnership altogether. God will do what God will do and my job is just to stay in his good graces.

God Needs Me?

Some time ago I learned about journaling with listening prayer. I discovered that I could ask God a question and begin journaling and it seemed like the process of writing made it easier to hear from him. One time during listening prayer and journaling, I was asking God a question. It was something like, "How would you like me to proceed in this arena of life?" As I was journaling, I wrote a bit about God needing me in some way. I stopped right there. I thought to myself, "Well I must not be hearing from God, because obviously he doesn't need me." You see, I was always taught that God doesn't need us. God is perfect in every way and he can do anything he wants. He didn't need me to create the world or put the stars in the sky. Why would he need me now? That doesn't make any sense. I'm not indispensable. I don't have any amazing talent. I could not have heard that God needs *me*! I was thinking like passive underdog.

Passive theology represents our attempt to embrace and acknowledge the sovereignty of God but not our paradoxical partnership with him. In its defense, it is our honor of God run-a-muck. We're surrendered but not responsible. The imbalance renders us impotent, superfluous and quite frankly, bored.

Quenching The Spirit

This assumption of our uselessness can block us from recognizing the prompting of the Holy Spirit. We never want to quench or grieve the Spirit. We know that Ephesians 4 says, "Do not grieve the Holy Spirit of God, with whom you were sealed for the day of redemption." But because of underdog's lack of understanding that he has a significant role to play in the story, he's not really *expecting* to be given much to do. Passive Christianity does not walk through a day expecting to be prompted. Why would he if he is not an active player in the story? Sensitivity to the prompting of the Holy Spirit is a skill that requires humility, practice and development. That development cannot take place unless one assumes he is being regularly called upon to participate. That development requires a measure of trial and error, all dependent on the original assumption that there is cooperation going on and that it is necessary. If we understood ourselves to be active players with God, we would pay closer attention to the seemingly "random" train of thought, to the coincidences and the gut senses.

Once on a Splankna training trip, we were getting some therapeutic massage (a favorite treat on training weekends). I felt a strong impulse from the Holy Spirit to tell the massage therapist I was chatting with that Jesus loves her. That felt understandably awkward and I hesitated. The longer I waited the harder it was to speak. I knew without a shadow of doubt that it was God's leading. Nonetheless, I didn't follow through. It breaks my heart that I missed an opportunity to represent the Lord. I apologized to my Father and prayed for her and for me. I prayed that I would have more courage the next time he called me. We often ask God to lead us, but are we willing to be led? In *The Forgotten God*, Frances Chan suggests that we are fooling ourselves into thinking that we want to be led by the Holy Spirit.[69] Underdog would rather warm the bench than get in the game. And the game is played in the smallest moments as much as it is on the grand stage. The Spirit is just as interested in a kind word spoken as a he is in global missions. He is equally active in national revivals and evening strolls. Don't wait for a vast undertaking to follow prompting. Start by following a whisper. In a sense, those small acts of social obedience are even more difficult than our grand gestures for the Kingdom. Faithfulness in little leads to faithfulness in much. If the Spirit cannot get us involved in the little ways, how can we be useful for the big ones?

Lip Service

The students shuffled around and eventually found their seats. My husband had just arrived for the first evening of his new class at Denver Seminary. Dr. Vernon Grounds was subbing in *The Philosophy of C.S. Lewis* and my husband couldn't wait. He's a big Lewis fan. (So are we, even though we just gave him a hard time). But rather than diving into the expected content, Dr. Grounds opened his lecture with an invitation. He asked the students to write down at least five things they knew about prayer. Then everyone took turns sharing what they had written. Soon the room was full of the beautiful descriptions and theological truths. The seminary students described, in poetic articulation, how prayer is "a direct line to God," "it can bring healing," "it brings supernatural wisdom and peace," and so on. When everyone was feeling sufficiently spiritual, he asked the room a startling question. "If you believe these things to be true about prayer, why don't you do more of it? Everyone fell silent.

So reader… get out a paper and pen. Seriously.

Ask yourself this question and write down the answer. I want you to see it. No one else will know but you and God. How much time have you really spent in prayer this week? Write it down and look at it for a minute.

If you're a normal Christian, you aren't particularly proud of that answer. It's pretty low isn't it? Why? We would all give prayer the same astounding definition—actually communicating with the Living God. And yet in arresting contradiction, we don't *do* it all that much. How can that be? What's behind this inconsistency?

Several years ago my husband and I were invited by a nearby Christian teaching organization to be a part of a live taping for an audio book. I was really excited about the topic: *Why our prayers are ineffective.* I'm just thrilled that someone is admitting this out loud. I couldn't wait to really explore the issue with other thinking believers. We said our hello's and settled in for the discussion. The group leader worked his way into the meat of the issue. He established this odd conundrum of our spoken belief in the power of prayer and our near dismissal of it as a real practice. He talked about how shocked he was when he first became a believer to find that while he couldn't wait to strike up a conversation with his newfound God, his fellow more "seasoned" brothers and sisters in Christ would pass on the invitation for prayer requests. "How could they have nothing to say to the open ear of God himself?" he wondered. Eventually he delivered his conclusion to the group: the reason the church doesn't pray is because she's lazy.

I started to squirm again.

I got that slight tremor that I've always had when the Spirit is nudging me to speak up. But this was not my meeting, not my evening. I was a guest. I didn't feel like it was quite my place to speak up in a live taping and essentially disagree with the main premise. But the Spirit doesn't care much about social mores and wouldn't relent. So up went my hand. "I don't think that's fair," I said, trying to be respectful. "I don't think laziness is the reason the church doesn't pray. I think she doesn't pray because she's lost hope."

Our Vicious Cycle

Like we've already mentioned, we love to quote James 5:16, "The prayer of a righteous man is powerful and effective." But deep inside, most of us don't feel like that's really true. We don't tend to experience our own prayers as powerful and effective, and yet the scriptures make this statement, so we secretly wonder, "Well then, maybe I'm not a 'righteous man.'" It seems that somewhere between Pentecost and today, a vicious cycle has developed in the Christian psyche. We do hear the occasional testimony of God moving in a profound supernatural way in response to prayer (especially in third world countries) but our more common experience seems like close to nothing happens when we pray. Now again, this is not something we say out loud. But privately, most of us do not approach a prayer with the honest expectation that because of it, something literal and measurable is going to happen. When we pray, it's more out of a type of group-think norm that it's what we *should* do. That it's the right thing, even if it doesn't produce much. We resort, for instance, in times of illness and injury to asking God to "be with the doctor's hands" as if he wasn't already.

Privately, we pray as a spiritual discipline
and corporately as a social courtesy.

Our vicious cycle looks like this: most of us have a lifetime of history with prayer that says nothing much happens when we pray. Yes, good things do happen in our lives. People recover from illness. Desperately needed money comes through at the last minute. Travel plans go off smoothly without incident and storms subside. But not in any different frequency or greater likelihood than for those who do not pray. Our prayers seem superfluous. Most of the time it seems like we're sending a message in a bottle that is just bobbing out there somewhere.

Subsequently, when we approach the next prayer opportunity, we do not honestly expect anything to happen that time either. We *say* we do. We *want* to believe something will happen, but our experience resists us. And we know what the Scripture says: "If a man prays and doubts, he should not expect to receive anything.[70] And *that* experience *does* ring true. If faith, in this example, is the honest expectation that our prayers carry weight, that something will *happen* because we pray, then we pray without faith, or at least without much faith. And when we pray without faith, nothing happens. Since nothing happens, our next prayer has even *less* faith, and on goes the cycle. We don't believe when we pray because our prayers don't work, and our prayers don't work because we don't believe when we pray!

Underdog is chasing his proverbial tail.

Let's say I was a chemist, and the conventional wisdom in my field teaches that every time you combine the liquid blue stuff with the liquid green stuff, it creates a big, sparkling explosion. If I tried that combination for the first time and nothing happened, I might chalk it up to error. But if I tried it 400 times over decades and the explosion never happened, it wouldn't be *rational* to come to trial number 401 with an honest expectation that something will explode. It would only be reasonable to lose "faith." Where can I come up with honest expectation against rationality? Underdog is stuck. He can't find partnership with the Lord, only futility.

From that position of futility, we are forced to come to several destructive conclusions about God. The biggies are, "It's not his timing," "It must not have been his will," or my personal favorite, "Everything happens for a reason." All of these theological propositions remove us as partners. They essentially call us pawns. The assumption behind these statements is that our role is insignificant. Rather than asking, "What could I have done differently? How might I be missing or avoiding my contributive role to play?" we just take a deep sigh and resign to the grand, disappointing "sovereignty" of God. We pray tiny, faithless prayers and when nothing happens we say, "See? Oh well."

So what can we do?

God does not seem to be solving this dilemma for us. It seems that the onus is on us. How do we break out of this cycle where we pray without believing so nothing happens, and since nothing happens, we continue to pray without belief? What would it take to throw a wrench into this vicious cycle? I think the real issue lies in our false understanding of *what's happening when we pray.*

Growing up I remember feeling so baffled by this idea. If God is perfect, all loving and all wise, then why do we need to pray? Isn't he going to do the best thing at every moment regardless? Is he going to make a poor choice unless I instruct him? Is he in a bad mood unless I plead with him? The covert message behind the childhood prayer theology passed down to me was that,

we pray to coax a reluctant God into action.

Why he is reluctant, no one addressed. It was apparent to me in my earliest examination of the Christian worldview that Scripture's description of what's real, and our experience, are far from congruent. If the mechanism behind prayer is that I'm coaxing a reluctant God into action, then what am I to conclude when the prayer seems "unanswered?" I only have a few despairing options. Either God "didn't move" because he doesn't want to, he isn't interested, or because I am somehow not approved of him, not worthy. Passive theology leaves us empty, devoid of partnership and discouraged.

I had a cherished evening all alone in my house, a very rare occurrence for a mother of three. It was a good thing too because I really needed some time alone with God. This was one of those times when my heart was fierce. I was fed up with a particular issue that he seemed to be ignoring. I had struggled and prayed for years and nothing was moving. I came to him angry that night. "God, I don't care how you do it. If you need to discipline me, tell me I'm wrong, give me an answer, anything. But deal with me on this God! Meet me! I don't care what you need to say to me. Just say *something*. Deal with me!" I railed at him, imploring for hours until I finally heard his reply. "There's more to your part than begging me," he said.

What?

I was stopped in my tracks. That was the first moment that I realized my own theological passivity. I had never even noticed it in my own heart, but it was true. I really *did* think that my only part was to beg him! I really did think that my part was to beg and if he didn't seem to answer then I needed to beg *harder.* I was so stunned that I had to ask, "There is? There's more to my part? What is it?" He wasn't talking about natural behaviors. I had exhausted every natural means I could to solve this particular issue. I had been plenty active. He was saying something about our relationship—something about prayer and partnership, but it would take me a while longer to understand.

In Chapter 14 we'll explore what he meant that night.

See No Evil

Passive theology bleeds into our dealings with the enemy as well. At the mention of Satan, the passive, underdog Christian closes his eyes, plugs his ears and says, "La, la, la." He denies that the spiritual realm actually exists. Even though the Bible mentions it over and over, he skips right over it into avoidance. Why? Because he's afraid. He doesn't know what to do. Passive thinking reasons that if we don't engage in any kind of battle then there really isn't one. You do realize that this works out just fine for Satan. Our passivity gives him an open door. Ignoring something doesn't make it go away. It doesn't change the fact that it is real. It just makes you unprepared when you *are* under attack. It's not only dangerous, it's irresponsible.

I remember when I first had my eyes opened to the reality of the spiritual realm. It was quite overwhelming. In fact, I remember thinking; "It was never this bad until I knew about it. I wish I never learned about warfare." I felt like I had mistakenly taken the red pill instead of the blue. I wanted to go back and bury my head in the sand. Of course, it doesn't work that way. Avoiding the spiritual realm is not productive. It doesn't give us the upper hand. There is no reason to ignore the battle that's already been won for us.

I couldn't believe my ears. My brother had been leading worship there for several years when he mentioned that the church building had a ghost. Yes. A ghost.

"What?" I asked incredulously. He explained how most of the leadership at this prominent, mid-sized church had seen, at different occasions over about ten years, an apparition of a little girl floating through the building's hallways late at night. She would appear at a distance, move around, look at you and then vanish. "Everyone knows about it," he explained, "especially the youth group, since they meet in the basement after hours." "Why on earth is it allowed to stay?" I asked. "I don't know," he said. "The leaders just try to keep it hush-hush." "So you're telling me that an evil spirit of some kind has been manifesting in your building for over ten years and no one's doing anything about it?" (My hackles were up.) "Let's get rid of it!" "How?" he asked.

I wish this was an unusual example, but it isn't. Scripture is clear that Satan is alive and active—that his cohorts are involved in our lives in real, tangible ways. But underdog would rather consider all of that to be metaphorical, just a vague representation of evil. My own theological background is a particularly sharp example of this type of denial. I remember what a revelation it was to first consider that not all of my thoughts were coming from me. I didn't realize until working with demonization in clients that I had grown up thinking of evil as conceptual but not literal. I could recite all of those biblical examples of Jesus dealing with demons as present, viable entities, but I guess I thought that was a feature of antiquity. That that sort of thing happened back then when things weren't civilized, but certainly not anymore.

In medicine and mental health, for example, we have surrendered the biblical, spiritual worldview in favor of diagnoses and medications. If the establishment has given it a title, it must not be spiritual. Passivity never considers a demonic element in schizophrenia, addiction or cancer. Evil is a metaphor.

See *Only* Evil

On the other hand, we're equally as passive when we see a demon under every rock. When we interpret every unpleasant event as a win for the dark side we're playing the underdog. If I attribute every stub of my toe and bad mood to the enemy's influence rather than normal life and fallenness, I create an enormous enemy and a tiny little God. In Romans 1:20, God states un-defensively that "man has no excuse" but to acknowledge the reality of his existence simply by the evidence of creation itself. To look to our right and left and conclude that this world is so profoundly evil is not only incorrect, it's sinful. Great laud and attribution to the enemy supposedly exhibited all around us is a form of worship. Only underdog sees the world through the adversary's eyes.

I was setting up camp when a park ranger came to our site with instructions on how to react if we stumble upon wildlife. She explained that with some animals we should make eye contact and walk away slowly. With others we should not make eye contact because to them it is a sign of aggression. With those types we should run away as fast as we can. All of this animal encounter training was fascinating but the most interesting part was her vivid description of how to react when you come across a bear. She told my family (including my small children) that with a bear we should attempt to make ourselves appear larger. She said we should make loud noises to fool the animal into thinking that we are the actual threat. I looked at my five year old and thought, "Good luck buddy."

How likely is it that a bear is going to be intimidated by a three-foot, 40 pound kid? We all know that if her ingenious plan doesn't work and the bear attacks, we are done for. But if the bear is gullible enough to be fooled by our ruse, we might actually have a chance. The bear has the upper hand, but I might be able to fool him into thinking otherwise.

I'm pretty sure the entities of the enemy go through similar training. Satan gets them all together and says, "Ok guys, these humans have no idea that the war is over and that we've already been defeated. Oh and get this…" (He leans in as if he's telling them some big secret and whispers with a chuckle) "…they don't really understand that they are ambassadors for Christ. So do your best to make your voice really loud and make yourself look bigger. Come off as big and bad as possible and maybe we can scare them into giving us more influence." And we buy it. We buy the lie that the enemy is big, bad and scary. But if the enemy is so big, what does that say about God? Someone has to be bigger. If we see Jesus as a passive wimp and Satan as a big, bad, scary monster, who wins?

Recently there's been a great deal of Christian press given to the idea that there are worldwide, clandestine organizations of the uber-powerful, rich and evil who are really running everything behind our backs. Supposedly they are calculating the governments, controlling global economy and lacing our media with subliminal messages. They are rumored to be behind all of the wars, the elections, the stock market and the school systems. They are the stealth force infiltrating everything from the Boy Scouts to the NFL.

Those who fall deeply into this thinking would probably give them credit for hurricane Sandy.

Of course the Mason's, for example, do exist and something like the Illuminati may as well, but why are we so impressed? Why do we think evil is so powerful? It's especially odd that we can believe that ordinary people, who put their pants on one leg at a time just like us, are pulling off super-human trickery.

Consider this: when we entertain these thoughts that secret evil is lurking around every corner, we are giving our focus, our homage, our (dare I say) worship to that evil. Over-focus is a form of worship. It *invites* the warfare. Scripture says in James "resist the devil, and he will flee from you." Are we resisting the enemy when we attribute so much to his activity? What is it about us that wants to think that grand impressive schemes are underway? I contend that it's because they *are*. But not in the enemy's camp. And one day soon, when every knee bows, we will finally be accurately impressed.

Don't Engage

Sometimes it's not that we think the enemy doesn't exist, or that evil's running everything, we just don't want to be the ones to deal with it. Can't someone else do that? Can't that just be the work of pastors and those specifically called to deliverance ministry? I mean, isn't that their job? When I first started learning that warfare was real, I needed to enter the battle for my son, but I was reluctant. He was 18 months old and for a while he had been having night terrors. He had begun to bang his head into the floor. He screamed without ceasing, no matter his mood. Things were progressively getting worse.

I had recently been seeing Sarah and learning about my authority in Christ. I would pray in the best way I knew how, but I always felt inadequate. Nonetheless, I couldn't ignore my son being tortured at night. I couldn't ignore my son hurting himself. I had to do something. I would pray and prayer would help, but I couldn't get his destructive behavior to stop for long. I made an appointment for Isaac to work with Sarah.

Three weeks later, on the day of our appointment, I had a demonic attack of my own. One of those dreams where you are awake but you can't move, all the while being threatened by the enemy. On the way to Isaac's appointment, the experience was on my mind. I wondered if we should work on me instead of Isaac. But I kept feeling that it was imperative that we focus on him. Besides, it could be three more weeks before Sarah would have an opening. I don't remember the details of his emotional work. But I do remember that we ended with a prayer to remove the enemy's influence and close those doors.

Afterward, I told Sarah about the attack on me. She suggested that it might be the enemy trying to get me to focus on myself rather than on Isaac. She said, "Did you notice that the threatening entity couldn't touch you?" I hadn't noticed. She explained what was accomplished at the cross, and the position of authority that I was given as one who is "in Christ." That was a turning point for me. I am covered in the blood of Jesus. I am a new creation in Christ. All the enemy had the right to do was threaten me. And I didn't let his threats distract me from Isaac's work. The Lord healed Isaac of all those symptoms that day. No more night terrors, no more banging his head into the floor and no more constant screaming. And he started me on a journey toward discovering my authority.

In Luke 10, Jesus sent out seventy-two of his followers. They returned to him with joy and said, "Lord, even the demons submit to us in your name." Jesus replied, "I saw Satan fall like lightning from heaven. I have given you authority to trample on snakes and scorpions and to overcome all the power of the enemy and nothing will harm you." I really don't think most of us grasp this. Jesus made us the bearers of his authority. The authority that holds him "far above all rule and authority, power and dominion, and every name that is invoked, not only in the present age but also in the one to come."[71] Jesus says, "You have all authority over the enemy," but passive theology says, "No, surely not. He's too big and I'm too small."

Playing Their Game

Someone gave me a book years ago that contained exhaustive lists of demonic names. Hundreds, maybe thousands of sinister titles, some of them simply sin categories like a "spirit of lust," some were formal names like "Mammon." Do all demons have names? Possibly. Scripture isn't definitive on that. But even if they do, it is a fallacy and a feature of underdog theology to think that we need to know those names in order to exercise dominion over them. Underdog Christian is playing their game when he thinks that way. He thinks that they hold the cards and that an evil spirit "doesn't have to leave" unless we use the perfect words against him. He interviews demons at length in order to ascertain the details of their presence, their right to be there and what it takes to remove them. In an attempt to accomplish deliverance, he is unwittingly honoring the demons not only by such meticulous attention to them, but by the assumption that they have him on an information leash. He's giving the enemy the upper hand.

Proponents of this deliverance paradigm will argue that Jesus himself asked for "Legion's" name in the process of casting him out. Yes, he did, but he gives us many more examples of removing them *without* details. The demons aren't holding the cards.

The truth is that *they* have to play *our* game.

They are the defeated ones and we are the ambassadors of Jesus' authority. The enemy can only remain based on a lack of detailed information if that's the right we give him. Words are only symbols of meaning. It is what we mean by what we say that carries weight. Think of it this way: if a particular spirit can only be removed if you properly name it "addiction," then how could someone who speaks Chinese ever remove him? Specific language is not a necessary incantation for handling the enemy. We don't have to worry about naming them by their requirement. It works the other way around. They have to play our game. They are bound to capitulate to *our* intention. Because we are the ones bearing the authority in Christ, they must respond to what *we* mean by what we say.

For example, let's look at the words "curse" and "hex." One believer might mean one thing by the word "curse" but another believer has a different definition. The enemy is not sitting back comfortably, waiting for the Christian to figure out what the kingdom of darkness means by the word "hex." He isn't saying, "Ha! Too bad. You said 'hex' but you really should've said 'curse.' Now I don't have to leave." It's the other way around. Whatever the bearer of authority means when he says 'hex' is what the enemy is bound to follow. *They are the underdogs.* In Chapter 14 we'll visit this further as well.

A Blessing For The Passive

Now it needs to be acknowledged before we continue that the great thing about the passive theological underdog is how deeply he holds respect and honor for God. Passive Christian carries deep awe for the sovereignty of the Lord. He would never have "Jesus is my homeboy" on the back of his t-shirt. UpperDog needs to retain that deep respect as he moves away from the rest of the passive position.

Theological Aggression

Rebel Dog

We can be theologically aggressive as well. One of the ways is in willful sin. Because underdog Christian doesn't really believe that God's standards of righteousness are his blessing, he attends church regularly, maybe even serves in a ministry, but refuses conviction and change. I have a very good friend, a godly man. He was raised in the church and has dedicated his life to the Lord. His family and ours came alongside each other in many ways. We taught together, we prayed together, we fought for the weak together. Our families were deeply bonded. I was so thankful that my children had another father figure and two godly men to look up to.

My friend's main struggle was with authority. Regularly I would encourage him to remember that he is an UpperDog. I had noticed that he didn't stand up for himself. He was too docile when he needed to be bold. He wouldn't hold anyone accountable. He was a great guy except for this area of weakness. I would try to speak truth and life into him, try to get him to embrace his strength, but I noticed that he kept falling into patterns of weakness.

This was baffling to me until the day he revealed to everyone that he had been living a double life. We were all dumbfounded. This man was a leader, counselor, prayer warrior, etc. He was raised in the church for heaven's sake. Yet he had so much secret sin that we all went into shock when it was revealed. My kids had called him Uncle! His inability to embrace his position in the Kingdom was really rooted in hidden guilt and shame. How can a man that so many people look up have been such an imposter? How did this happen? How could this have been going on for decades and no one knew?

I realized he couldn't be the UpperDog that God created him to be, because he was full of shame and rebellion. We talk about how all sin is the same, and that's true in terms of grace and salvation. But sometimes we want to default to those Scriptures to excuse behavior. I couldn't shake the feeling that this kind of sin was different—it seemed worse somehow. Is it because it was secret?

I just kept going back to God for answers. God started to teach me about the difference between sin and fundamental rebellion. We all sin. We fall and repent and work to move forward. But this man was not willing to engage in that process of maturation. He was not receptive to conviction. He knew exactly what he was doing and he chose it anyway. He chose the sin, year after year without repentance. He chose rebellion flagrantly and repetitively. We can justify our sin. We can keep it a secret. But the problem is that it morphs into rebellion against the spirit of God. We cannot do that and be UpperDogs. We have to choose.

Jesus tells us that it is better to enter eternity without an eye or a limb than to continue to sin to the point of rebellion. No one is perfect. No one is without sin, but you *can* be without rebellion. Sin happens, but we can stay humble, honest and open to conviction. Even though sin lingers, we can maintain a posture that pursues greater righteousness. We are not saying this is easy, it's not. Being a Christian is tough. It's counterintuitive to our fallen human nature. But neither can we be like Christ and continue to be abusive and unloving towards family or stubbornly refuse to work on ourselves until our mate changes. We cannot go on justifying sexual sin, addiction and other things contrary to the nature of God.

If you are in rebellion, there is a part of you that knows it: you might just refuse to admit it. Whatever it is, it's not worth it! I promise you. You cannot put a price on a clean conscience. Knowing that you are where God wants you to be is precious. Fighting to do what is right fills your heart like nothing else. I am constantly asking God to show me the plank in my own eye. I want to see my sin before it becomes rebellion. He is faithful to meet me in that request and he'll meet you too. Aggressive underdog engages in sin and demands that grace abound. But UpperDog invites the searching eye of the Lord into the secret places. He can afford to because he knows he is the apple of his father's eye.

Christian Witchcraft

We've discussed how Passive Underdog can end up living like a pawn, a mere observer of the sovereign moves of God with no significant role to play. I think this is the more common imbalance we see. But because of the difficulty of partnership and the intrinsic, dynamic tension there, we can also fall off the other side of the wagon. We can end up on the *aggressive* side of theology. We do have a significant role to play in this life. We represent a real variable in what happens, but we can get confused about the mechanisms. Our attempt to harness our significance can also go awry. Passive theology misses partnership on one side and aggressive theology misses it on the other. Aggressive theology says that *we* are the ones running the show.

The Tony Robbins' and Suze Ormans' of the world have beaten us to this punch. The "positive thinking" movement has swept the secular landscape with *their* answer to the question of our role in the story. Tony raked in 30 million dollars in 2007 alone and has impacted approximately four million people from 100 countries around the world.[72] Norman Vincent Peal, Napoleon Hill, the speakers in "The Secret" and many others have gathered an astounding following. What's the hook? "Positive thinking creates." And they're right. It does. God made it that way. (We'll explore that in detail in Chapter 14). But as he does with all truths, the enemy takes a reality designed for God's purposes and distorts it for his own.

The world has taken this recognition that thought has substance and morphed it into our current-day version of the original temptation: "You can be like god."[73] Positive thinking teachers claim that with the power of your thoughts, you can manifest anything you want out of this life. They dismiss the sovereignty of God. The secular positive thinking guru preaches that if you just learn to harness the power of positive thinking, you can have the life you've always wanted. Health, wealth, fame and love are at your fingertips. Just think positively. Put your intention out there into the universe and it will give you back what you desire.

They even go so far as to say that if you're driving to work and thinking, "I'm going to be late. I'm going to be late," then you will manifest that and be late. But if you drive to work thinking "I'm going to make it," then you will. They give no consideration to the fact that while I may be thinking my positive brains out, the guy in the car ahead of me could still be thinking, "I'm going to be late!" They don't realize that they're creating an inconsistent view of reality. They're making each one of us unilaterally sovereign. They're saying that every little thing that has ever happened to you was a result of your expectations—the intention you were putting out into the universe. Every time you got a hangnail or missed a promotion it was because subconsciously you *chose* it, and consequently it manifested.

New Age thinking teaches that you have the potential to simply become conscious of your expectations and the intentions you're sending out into the universe, and you can manifest better things on purpose. You can manifest anything you want. You don't have to be a Christian to see the fallacy in this proposition. We cannot all be unilaterally running the universe. Even if my intention carries weight, so does the person's standing next to me. My intention bumps up against everyone else's.

But the mechanism they're referring to is real. What they are observing in the created fabric is accurate. God *did* design our intention to carry weight, to impact reality,

But for his purposes, not ours.

Scripture explains that God is sovereign. His sovereignty is a rich concept. It means many things too lofty for this book and for my brain. But in this context it means that God has not given us all potential. He has made us active players, meaningful partners but he remains the boss. He did not wire us with weighty intention so that we could "manifest" a $100 bill whenever we feel like it. The only lie that is effective is the one that's mostly true. This is a terrific example. The problem with the positive thinking movement and movements like "The Secret," etc., is not that their understanding of the power of thoughts is incorrect, just their understanding of *how much* and *why*. Later we'll look at how intention is meant to operate in partnership with God.

I wish I didn't have to, but I must level this same accusation at the Christian community as well. The church has developed her own version of this imbalance. Again, we mean well. We want to live our Christianity and not just think about it. We want to take it seriously. We read the promises in Scripture and we attempt to put them into practice. Aggressive underdog can recognize the tragedy of passivity in the church and he's knocking himself out to be more impassioned, more involved. But true, productive involvement in the story, true partnership with God is fraught with tension and paradox. It's vulnerable and non-formulaic. It is so many things that our fallen nature reviles. It requires a constant balancing of our involvement with his sovereignty and that's difficult and counterintuitive. So in our attempt to combat passivity, we sometimes end up going too far in the other extreme: aggressive theology.

We've called it many things, "Name it and claim it," "Word of Faith," "Health and Wealth Gospel," but at its heart lies the teaching that God wills all Christians to have pleasure and comfort and that we need only to speak it out loud and it will come true. The idea is that we are each individually the decisive variable in how well the promises of God are appropriated in our lives. Well-known preachers in many different generations have amassed great fortunes (and sometimes great prison sentences) through this theology. Naïve believers longingly stare into television screens promising them healing or needed financial assistance or a relationship restored if they will just speak it in faith (or worse, give money to the preacher).

Aggressive theology wields a prayer much like a weapon. The underlying message is that God is obligated by our prayers, that my declaration in Jesus' Name is sovereign itself. The subtle logic goes like this: Since I am "in Christ," I "have whatever I ask in his name." So the only variables in play are my own measures of faith and holiness. My holiness is my right to what I ask, and my faith is my power to command it. In its defense, this *is* an attempt to embrace our role in the story rather than to live like pawns. But it has gone too far. It has just tipped the scale in the other direction. It is fundamentally manipulative. It uses Scripture to remove God's own will from the equation. I hate to say it, but it is our version of witchcraft. I'll tell here again a story I shared in the Splankna book:

My client and I were saying hello at the opening of session. As she spoke, I noticed that the pinky on her right hand was bent. "What happened to your pinky?" I asked her. She started to tell me how she and her husband were painting their living room a few years ago and she was climbing a ladder. Suddenly she stopped, visibly irritated with herself and said, "No, no. In Jesus' Name, this pinky is whole!" But the pinky was not whole. Her statement was neither true, nor powerful. It was irrational, demanding and empty. Her theology was that if she "spoke" it with enough force and frequency, the pinky would have to comply.

We discussed at length in the first book of this series, *Splankna: Redeeming Energy Healing For The Kingdom of God*, what it is that defines a witchcraft posture. Considering the many biblical examples of God either endorsing or commanding things that we would now consider witchcraft—like rituals, words of power, meaningful objects, symbols etc., we must be clear about what makes witchcraft witchcraft. It is not the behavioral constructs themselves but the posture of heart. Witchcraft is the demand for special power or special knowledge.[74] It is the attempt to make oneself sovereign, to say, "I will have no limits. I will have what I desire." When we embrace aggressive theology and use Scripture to excuse our demands, we are fashioning "Christian Witchcraft."

Yes, Jesus does tell us that our words carry weight, our faith can move mountains and that we have what we ask in his name. But Scripture also tells us that the Lord God remains sovereign. God also says that while "the lot is cast into the lap, its every decision is from the Lord,"[75] and that "it is the Lord who works out everything to its proper end," and that "while in their hearts humans plan their course, it is the Lord who establishes their steps."[76] And one of our favorites, "God works out all things for the good."[77] Who works everything out? Us? By our "word of faith?' No. It is the Lord God who remains sovereign even considering the remarkable and undeserved role he has given us in the story. Yes, we affect things with our words, our expectations, and our intentions. But we are not the only variable. Contributors yes, sovereign no. Health and wealth theology is our version of idolatrous witchcraft tucked inside a pretty, leather Bible cover.

Declaration Paranoia

Because the aggressive Christian does understand that words are constitutive, that they create, he can be vulnerable to obsessive thinking and paranoia around this idea. The Christian who panics if they ever accidentally say, "I feel sick," is falling into obsessiveness. Because we naturally long for control, for answers and guarantees, we can end up using our "declaration" power not just to manipulate God, but to control our own lives as well. I've heard many a well-intended believer scold someone for "confessing" a negative word. But even in this there needs to be balance. Yes, our words are powerful. God made them to carry weight. We'll explore that in much more depth in Section 4. But again, we are not sovereign. My powerful words do carry impact, but they are not solely, independently creative. They do not unilaterally reign. They are a *contribution*. They impact things as a variable, not a sledgehammer. Of course we should attend to our words. Of course we should seek to generally speak life and grace over everything, but as a growing general posture of maturity, not in a terrified underdog posture that believes that saying, "I'm tired" is an unconscionable curse.

A Back-Handed Thank You

Another example of aggressive theology is the misuse of gratefulness. Aggressive underdog "thanks" God for what was just requested, but more as a weapon than an offering. There is confusion about the role of gratefulness in the story. The skewed theology sounds something like this: If we thank God for something before it comes to be, it causes it to happen. Again, the act of giving thanks is done more like a demand for God's goodness than a response to it. Like the "thank you Lord" seals the deal. It *has* to happen now. This kind of faux gratefulness is only another style of attempted manipulation. I remember a fellow believer defending this practice based on "calling things that are not as though they are."[78] But in context, I think that scripture is referring more to imagination and expectation than demand. It may seem like too fine a line to squabble with, but fine or not it is critical. Witchcraft is the demand for special knowledge and power outside of God. Demand clothed in "thank you" is still a witchcraft heart posture.

Genuine gratefulness is another story, even when something is yet to come about. We'll talk about that in Chapter 14.

Tragic Conclusions

Look at the logical conclusion from this prayer theology. Because aggressive underdog *does* think he's sovereign and he backs it up with Scripture, he doesn't know what to think when a prayer doesn't bear fruit. When the illness doesn't heal or the divorce is finalized, when the foreclosure is signed or the pregnancy fails. Aggressive theology preaches that if you pray and don't see a result, it's because your faith is insufficient. It is your personal failure. They have taught that because it is God's general will that healing (for instance) take place, his answer is always "yes" in every circumstance. He's just waiting for you to appropriate it. So if your prayer did not produce the desired result, it must be due to your weakness in faith. You didn't *really* believe. Because if you had...

The other devastating attribution that is made inside of aggressive theology is that of "hidden sin." If you prayed in faith and your prayer was not productive (i.e. God said "no"), then you must be in some hidden sin that's blocking God's favor. This confusion was around in Jesus' day as well. In John 9:2, he was asked about a man who was born blind. "Who sinned, this man or his parents?" Jesus explained that neither the man's sin nor that of his parents was to blame for the man's blindness but that it was the sovereign decision of the Lord for the purpose of exhibiting his own glory. Here the clear implication is that the man's blindness was not due to the lack of faith in those that had surely prayed for him, nor was it due to anyone's sin. The Lord had his own plan in play. This is not to say that sin in one's life never stands in the way of blessing or effectiveness. It certainly can. But in that case it is a variable, not a calculation.

A third conclusion can also be seen through the lens of the aggressive underdog: the failure of God. This was my second visit to the mother and daughter team of intercessory prayer ministers. I was deep in the throes of processing a childhood trauma—my parent's divorce. In the second grade I had a good friend, Denise, whose parents got divorced. I distinctly remember thinking to myself, "Whew! I'm so glad I don't ever have to worry about that. After all, Christians don't get divorced." So when my own parents' marriage began to fall apart at the seams, I prayed. I was certain that God would not allow two believers, who both loved him and wanted the marriage to work, to end up separating. So when he did allow it, I felt betrayed. God failed. He did not come through and save the day like I was sure he would. God could have changed their hearts. He could have caused them to love each other. They were both praying! But he didn't. He allowed everything to fall apart when we all know he "hates divorce." He betrayed his own edict and he failed us all.

As I sat under the ministry of these two fellow believers, I was bringing this bitterness before the Lord. I was pouring out my anger and accusation at how he withheld rescue, didn't answer prayer, how he messed up. Suddenly I heard his words as clear as day: "You *still* think you know how that should've gone," he said. I was stunned. I didn't realize until that moment that I had been believing all my life that God had failed in that situation. I had never considered that he might have done the *best* thing by allowing their divorce. I had never considered all of the variables at his disposal.

If the mechanism behind prayer is a simple one-to-one—I ask and God either does it or not—then I have to land in one of these camps. God is perfect. No Christian argues that. So if he doesn't "move" in response to my prayer, I only have a few conclusions to draw if I live in underdog theology. It's either because of some fault in me or because my request is not "his will." How much despair has been born of this confusion? If our theological framework says that all prayer requests with adequate holiness and faith will be realized as expected, then our only logical conclusion in the face of "unanswered prayer" is that either we failed or he did.

And we wonder why we aren't more devoted to prayer.

Aggressive theology represents our attempt to employ our role as partners without remaining under the sovereignty of God. It says that God is obligated by my prayer or declaration. It starts out with guns blazing but often leaves us humiliated and hopeless.

Aggressive In Warfare

Underdog Christian can also get aggressive in warfare. He thinks that dealing with the enemy is a "power encounter." He thinks he has to be bigger, louder and more intimidating than the demon in order to remove it. He thinks he has to out-power and out-smart the enemy. He runs long, intense, dramatic deliverance sessions with screaming, retching sufferers into the wee hours of the morning. Fierce command is his style and the Name of Jesus his bludgeon. He's got a very big Satan so he has to be bigger still. He's trying so hard to be strong. He's read the account of the seven sons of Sceva in Acts 19, where the demon confesses that he knows Paul and he knows Jesus. Aggressive underdog hopes they know his name too. He's not wrong for that, just over-compensating.

All Bark

Without realizing it, the aggressive underdog is taking on the enemy's own characteristics when dealing with him. We are out of line when we pick a fight with a demon. Calling names, taunting, threatening or torturing demons is not only counter-productive, it's sinful. "Fight fire with fire" is the wrong approach. When we act like bullies in the name of Jesus, we are aligning with them, not him. In Jude 1:9, we're told that only foolish men pick fights with the enemy. "Even the archangel Michael" did not dare slander the devil, but said instead, "The Lord Jesus rebuke you!"

I love the analogy of the NBA referee. Let's call him David and pretend that he's 5 feet, 5 inches tall, weighing 160 pounds. The average professional basketball player, on the other hand, is about 6 feet, 7 inches tall and weighs 224 pounds. There is no question here. The player is the one with the power. He towers over David the referee and can be quite intimidating, especially when he disagrees with the call, dripping sweat and probably profanity. So does the ref try to prove himself against this Goliath? Does he challenge the player to a battle of strength? Does he say, "Oh yeah? You want some of this?" Of course not. He doesn't have to. If he makes a call against a defiant player there is no power encounter involved. It is simply a legal encounter. Regardless of strength, intimidation or threat, one of them has the authority and the other does not. They do not have a power encounter, they have a legal one. It is actually the pocket-sized ref who has the upper hand and he doesn't need to prove it. The same applies to us in dealing with the enemy. When UpperDog really understands his authority, when he has his head and heart fully wrapped around it, there is no need for volume or drama. Grounded authority is quiet.

I'm Really Under Attack

Yet another way that we play the underdog with warfare (and I'm liable to step on some toes here) is when rather than denying or ignoring the enemy's involvement, we take pride in the dramatic level of warfare in our lives. We strut around; subtly proud of ourselves for the great oppression we're under. You know you've heard it, or maybe even said it yourself. It sounds something like this: "Wow, we're really under attack. We must be doing something great for the Kingdom!" or, "You wouldn't believe how hard the enemy tried to keep me from coming to this conference! He must really not want me to come." "Yes, the book-writing is going great but you wouldn't believe the warfare!"

There are two critical problems with this perspective. The first is the pride itself. Statements like those are subtly saying, "I'm really important to God, really critical or the enemy wouldn't be bothering with me. If you're not experiencing this level of warfare you're probably not quite as significant as I am."

It is also saying that there is a one-to-one connection between one's efficacy in the Kingdom and the level of warfare experienced. It's saying that the heavens are set up in such a way that the enemy can do whatever he wants. Subsequently, he can target the daylights out of the threatening ones and ignore the lazy ones. But this is not the case. Think about it for a moment. Follow it out to its logical conclusion. If that were true, if the warfare in one's life increases commensurate to his efficacy in the Kingdom, then we've already lost. There could never be someone like Billy Graham or Mother Teresa. People so threatening to the kingdom of darkness would've been taken out long ago. Their lives would've been fraught with peril, tragedy, illness and torture to the point that they could no longer function. And if this were true, if Kingdom effectiveness equals warfare, why on earth would anyone want to engage the Christian life? If this is the case then the enemy wins! I'm out. Game over. This theological travesty has taken out an incredible number of believers. But who would blame them?

Now I'm not saying you're free of warfare. I'm not saying that the perception of attack is false (although it may be). You may actually be experiencing a good deal of enemy influence in your life.

But it is not due to your importance to the Kingdom.

It is not because you're threatening. Everyone is threatening to the enemy. It is not something to be proud of and it is not your "cross to bear." It is not just what naturally has to be tolerated in the Christian life. If you're experiencing a great deal of warfare it's most likely because you have left a door open somewhere and you need to attend to your housekeeping. It is not a point of pride but a sign of something amiss. We'll pick up that discussion in chapter 11.

A Blessing For The Aggressor

Let's acknowledge the strength in the aggressor as well. Aggressive Christian is passionate and courageous. He really wants to participate, to get in the game and take God up on his promises in Scripture. He's a fighter and a risk taker. UpperDog would do well to retain those qualities too.

Downward Dogs (again)

Why do we succumb to passivity and aggression with God? For all of the same reasons we do culturally (plus a few more).

Jesus As Underdog

I saw a passion play at a little church in the Midwest. The man who played Jesus looked like a gaunt P.O.W. Right away I was disappointed with the visual image of Jesus. But that wasn't what bothered me the most. In the play, when the actor was in the garden of Gethsemane, he performed a very disturbing impression of Jesus. He was praying to the Father about the cup being taken from him, and in his depiction of this pivotal moment in Jesus' life, this actor screamed at God. He violently railed at God to take the cup from him, as if he desperately wanted to be free of the weight of bearing our sins. He portrayed Jesus like a child being forced to do something, shrieking and rebelling against his parent. He presented the heart of Jesus as if he wasn't at all willing to make the sacrifice but was *only* obligated. He disparaged the heart of Jesus and his desire to save us. He portrayed Jesus as a coward, as frail, overcome with terror and rebellion.

At the time I was confused. Why would they think that a portrayal of a cowardly, rebellious Jesus was accurate? The more I've pondered it the more I realize that it's part of the passive Christian's theology. But why? Jesus is no coward! Jesus is a warrior. Jesus fought the biggest battle of all and he did it with himself as the only weapon.

We can misunderstand Jesus as passive because we don't understand the nature of love. We don't get that love comes in many forms. We only see love in the kind, compassionate form, gentle and affectionate. But love is also fierce. When Jesus turned over those tables, he was full of righteous anger and love was still his primary motivation. Love saw the injustice. Love fights for the weak.

We tend to overlook the Scriptures when Jesus addresses the Pharisees as a "brood of vipers" and "white-washed tombs." What about when he looks at Peter and says, "Get behind me Satan!" Does that make you think of Jesus as passive? Jesus had balance. We need balance as well. I challenge you as you go through this book. Meditate on the Scriptures that show Jesus in the way you've been missing. Jesus is no wimp.

He Buries His Talents

Part of the reason we're underdog's with God is because we're afraid of failure. Fear plays a big part in our lives. The human specimen is painfully self-conscious. I could even fear you and what you will think of this book. Most of us fear judgment. We fear being misled and saying something that isn't true. I fear missing the plank in my eye when I notice the speck in my brother's eye. I'm afraid of missing my calling in some way and messing up the whole Kingdom (as if that were possible). Fear can paralyze and overwhelm us. It's one of the enemy's greatest tools. It's one of the biggest reasons we're passive. We convince ourselves that it's better not to move than to make a mistake. Better to hide than be found inadequate.

My daughter is a perfect example. She loves to play softball. I coached her the first year and I realized she had some natural talent. She had a great arm and was able to hit any pitch. She had confidence and loved the sport. But for some reason we skipped a season and when she returned the next year she wasn't so confident. She no longer believed in herself. In fact she almost quit. I encouraged her to keep going. I thought maybe she just needed some time to get back into the game. Then one practice I stayed around to observe. I watched her go up to bat and miss one ball after another. I asked her coach if I could talk with her. She came to the fence and looked at me with defeat and tears in her eyes. She wanted to quit. She wanted to bury her talents, and maybe she already had. I looked her in the eyes and said, "Maya, you know how to hit the ball. You are a great batter but what you don't have is confidence. Somewhere along the line you stopped believing in yourself." We said a prayer that God would fill her with confidence and remind her of her skill. She went back to bat and began to hit some of the pitches. During the season she hit a double and brought three girls home. She was remembered for that hit.

Maya was almost defeated. She almost gave in and buried a skill. If she had, I think it would have impacted her future. She would have learned to give up, and that burying a talent is an option.

My friend described this moment. The movie was over and everyone was motionless in reflective silence. The entire theater had been impacted by the message of the movie. That's when he heard God's voice, "Stand up and tell them the good news. Tell them there's hope." "What?!?" he whispered in a panic. Practically in tears and overwhelmed with fear and nervousness, he hesitated. Fervently, God implored him, "Stand up and tell them the good news. You can do it. They're ready. Their hearts are open."

What did he do? Nothing. He did nothing. He couldn't do it. Sadly, he buried his talent. This is a man who preaches every Sunday. As he told me this story, his sadness was palpable. "Why couldn't I just do it?"

Chances are, you and I might have done the same thing.

The question isn't whether or not we've ever hidden our gifts or shrunk back from shining, because I'm sure we all have at times. We all have moments of fear and doubt. We aren't perfect and we are going to fail sometimes. The true question is, are you characterized by it? Do you continually live your life hiding, playing it safe? It's time to get the shovels out and dig up those talents

Section 4

UpperDog Partners

*"I shook my fist at Heaven
and said, "God, why don't You do something?"
He said, "I did, I created you!""*

-Matthew West

So what *is* our part in the story? What is our role to play as sidekicks? We don't want to be mere theorizers of the Gospel. We want to be practitioners of it. We want to learn to cooperate well. This discussion has to begin with summarizing what we've already established about our historical abuses. As we've discussed, when the church has approached the question of our part in the story, we have generated two destructive extremes. We have to look these squarely in the face and clear them off of the table in order to start a fresh conversation.

The Extremes

It's just in our nature. We want things to be black and white. But that's not the fabric of reality. God's story is chock-full of dynamic tension: two truths that appear to be in contradiction and have to be navigated in constant balance. Think about how many of these we have to wrestle with:

Free will vs. predestination
Grace vs. works
The now and the not yet
The truth in love
Lose your life to find it
The last shall be first

We are constantly strained with truth-tensions. The contrast won't resolve. God has built tension and paradox into reality and we'd rather poke out our left eyes than tolerate it. The landscape of faith is no exception. The truth is that when it comes to faith and our part in the story, we have another dynamic tension. Two apparent contradictory realities are in play:

1. God is sovereign.
2. He has made us meaningful contributors.

He says things like, "Be my hands and feet," and "Your faith has made you well," implying that things are up to us. But then he also says that nothing escapes his sovereign lordship. He says things like, "Choose this day whom you will serve."[79] But he also says, "Whom I have chosen I have also predestined."[80] Dynamic tension. Constant apparent contradiction that has to be actively navigated. It's like walking a tightrope. Passivity and aggression are both easier to navigate than true partnership. Because this tension is so frustrating, the Church has developed two false theological "resolutions" to the problem. We've knocked ourselves out to land on one side of the faith tension or the other so we can escape the difficulty of the balancing act. It looks something like this:

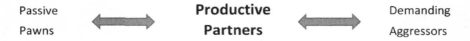

| Passive | | **Productive** | | Demanding |
| Pawns | | **Partners** | | Aggressors |

We'd rather be passive or aggressive than tolerate the tension because passivity and aggression are easier than partnership.

These two extremes play off of each other as well. The Christian pawns cannot handle even the suggestion that their faith could've been a variable. "How dare you suggest that God didn't heal so-and-so or change this or that situation because of my lack of faith!" It is deeply offensive. They know that the aggressors on the other side of the scale can be abusive with that accusation, so they won't have even a hint of it. But they don't realize that in their offense at the opposite abuse they are saying that their faith is no variable at all. That it *can't* be a variable. They are contending that their own measure of faith is inconsequential—that it had nothing to do with the fruit (or lack thereof) of the prayer. Do we really mean to say that when it is clearly unbiblical? Are we really willing to argue that our faith *can't* be a variable? It's *impossible* that my faith was weak and rendered my prayer less useful? I'm the pillar of all faith and belief? I don't think that's a position we can defend. What would we do with Jesus saying things like, "May it be done to you according to your faith," or "Your faith has healed you?"[81]

On the other hand, the aggressors contend that our faith is the *only* variable—that God's own involvement is what's irrelevant, not because his desire isn't important, but because it's static. Aggressors think they know his will in every situation and he's just waiting on us to believe and speak it into reality. Many a discouraged believer has been emotionally abused by the accusation, "You didn't believe."

Neither of these positions is productive. Neither one is honoring to God or advancing the Kingdom in our day. It isn't useful to lay down under his sovereignty or to dismiss it. It's time to embrace the dynamic tension, the "both-and." Scripture describes a joint enterprise, an interplay, a mysterious dance in which we are assigned real efficacy and responsibility in this story, while the sovereignty of God remains intact. Both-and. I am not god. He is not obligated by my "word of faith." And yet my faith remains a real, literal, substantive variable. Lively, frustrating, glorious, dynamic tension.

Let's explore it together.

Partnership with God comes in many flavors. Here we'll look at how we partner with God in these four ways:

In *Authority*
In *Creativity*
In *Obedience*
In *Prayer*

Partnering in Authority

"In those early centuries of Christianity,
Christians did not go out into the world apologizing.
They went to slay the powers of darkness
and undo the works of the devil
and they lived in holy triumph."
-John G. Lake

Authority is one of the central structures of the universe. Everything is ordered and there can be no order outside of authority. The canon of Scripture begins and ends with the issue of authority. When God crafted the crown of his creation, man in his own image, he placed Adam and Eve in the garden and said, "Now, take dominion." He didn't just say, "So what do you think of the digs? Pretty great, right? Since you're free of sin and in perfect communion with me, just relax. Hang out and enjoy yourselves." No. He said they had a job to do. They were to actively take ownership of their sphere of influence. They were to name the animals, craft structure, multiply and cultivate the earth. *Imago Dei* is meant to reign. God is fundamentally authoritative and when he made his own image, he also assigned that same characteristic. We are beings of authority.

Every person is given by God a sphere of influence—a personal kingdom over which to reign. Some of us have large kingdoms that encompass companies, government seats or even nations. Some have only the kingdom of their own body over which to exercise their authority, and there is every example in between. But all of us are reigning.

When the fall occurred, human kind was demoted. The enemy gained a measure of authority over the earth and over us because of our concession to sin. Satan enjoyed his promotion until the cosmos-shattering statement was uttered, "It is finished." At that point, the enemy lost that stolen measure of authority and we got it back. "Take dominion" is once again our assignment. Jesus defeated the enemy, sin and death at the cross, and then he was seated at the right hand of the Father, in dominion and authority "far above all rule and authority and power and dominion and every name that is named, not only in this age but also in the age to come."[82] He is the ultimate authority now. And we have also been "raised up and seated with him in Christ Jesus."[83]

What this means for UpperDog Christian is that we not only have natural authority over our little kingdoms, as do all who carry his image, we also carry the authority of Jesus into the world and into the heavens. We are even his representatives in the kingdom of darkness. When the enemy sees you, he sees the authority of Jesus resting on you.

A woman who came to Christ after living in the world of Satanism gave an interesting account of this. She shared that people who advance in dark arts commonly gain the ability to see into the spiritual realm. They can visibly see things like demonic attachments, angelic activity and the blood of Jesus covering a believer. She said that a skilled Satanist can spot a Christian from across a crowded room because they carry a huge mantle over them of power and authority in Jesus that is visible in the spiritual realm. "But we never worried much about that," she said "because we hardly ever met a Christian who knew how to use it."[84]

Now if that doesn't make something in you get fierce, you need to be resuscitated.

I mean, isn't that incredible? People aligned with Satan can see the latent power and authority resting over us, but most of us don't use it! We want to be exceptions to that rule and we want you to be also. So what does it look like to embrace our authority over the enemy without being paranoid or aggressive? It looks like handling your house.

Handling Your (Dog)House

I recall a moment with my daughter when she was three or four years old. She told me there were monsters in her room. I said, "Maya, you can tell them to leave." "I can?" she replied. I said "Sure. Just say, 'In Jesus name, leave.'" With excitement she said, half questioning, half eager "I can do that!?" I smiled and said "Yep." She said it with authority and a huge smile spread across her face. When I asked if the monsters had left, she said with amazement, "Yes!" From that point on, my daughter knew what she could do in the name of Jesus.

In Luke, Jesus says, "I praise you Father, Lord of heaven and earth, because you have hidden these things from the wise and learned, and revealed them to little children."[85] As my child, I authorized Maya to take authority over her room and anything in it. Maya did this when she commanded the monsters out of her room. Even she, as one of the smallest in the Kingdom, was able to handle her little house.

There's a whole host of excellent books on how to deal with warfare. We aren't going to reinvent that wheel. We're just going to discuss a posture toward warfare that avoids both passivity and aggression and opts for UpperDog-ness, (Yes, we're going to keep ridiculously conjugating that term.)

UpperDog understands that it is a legal universe. Satan is neither omnipotent nor omnipresent and neither are his emissaries. They are on a specific leash from God himself. Because of the cross and the empty tomb, the enemy has lost the upper hand. He has lost his fundamental right to us. We came out from under the law of sin and death.[86] Since the cross, the enemy can only do what he finds legal right to do because he no longer has authority. He finds rights through sin of all sorts because in our sin we are inadvertently agreeing with him, aligning with him, inviting him. Once we become aware of those subtle alignments we can repent and remove the enemy's influence. But it is imperative to remember that nothing is ever about warfare. Yes, I meant to say that. Nothing is ever about warfare. Everything the enemy does is just happening because of some loophole we've provided, some open door he's found through which to influence us. And that open door is a heart issue, not a demonic one. The activity of the enemy is always secondary to the heart issue. Always.

"But what about Job?" I can hear you contending. Even in the circumstance where God allows the enemy a particular freedom, it is still only because God has some purpose in mind. Not because the enemy can do whatever he wants, or has out-maneuvered God. Still a heart issue. It is certainly the prerogative of the Lord to use the enemy for his own purposes. But those purposes are still about our hearts. The enemy and his activity never deserve center stage.

UpperDog knows that he never needs to focus on the enemy. He knows that he only needs to attend to his own kingdom and the enemy loses hold. In Christ, we grow in aligning more and more with Jesus' own mind, his own will, and over time the enemy has less and less opportunity to influence us. One of the most destructive lies the enemy has ever devised is that warfare increases with Kingdom effectiveness. The truth is the exact opposite. The only way one can be increasingly effective in the Kingdom is with increasing intimacy with Jesus, faith and righteousness. These are the very things that diminish the enemy's ability to influence us not increase it. The more Kingdom effectiveness, the less warfare. If you find that not to be true, it's because you're believing the lie that your effectiveness equals warfare and the belief itself is the invitation, not your effectiveness.

I had been taking my son to my sister Tiffany's house so she could babysit while I worked. She had recently moved to the apartment across the hall. In this new place, Isaac was afraid. As soon as I parked the car and Isaac knew where we were, he would start to fuss. Isaac would cling to me, cry and beg me not to leave him. He would have a full-blown tantrum. This wasn't like him. Other than his parents, his Aunt Tiffany was his favorite person in the world. Tiffany and I were both perplexed. So one day on the way to my sister's house, I asked my two year old why he didn't want to stay there anymore. He said plainly, "There are monsters at Tiffy's." I said with determination, "Oh really!" When we got to my sister's, I told her what Isaac had disclosed and requested that we pray together to "clean up" her apartment. Isaac was clinging to me as usual and I said to him, "Let's make the monsters leave."

We came before the Lord and listened. We invited him to bring to mind anything that we needed to confess and repent of that was related to this disturbance. We attended to the ideas that came to mind. Then we simply took authority over the apartment. We cast out the warfare and dedicated the place to the Kingdom. We weren't loud or intense, just clear. Voila! Isaac said, "Thanks mom, monsters are gone" kissed me, jumped down and went to play. No more monsters. As it should be.

In Luke, Jesus encourages us, "Do not rejoice that the spirits submit to you, but rejoice that your names are written in heaven." This Scripture is a reminder of primacies. Do not mistake the authority Christ has given us with what is most significant and immeasurable. Our names are written in the book of life. We belong to Jesus! Keep your eyes fixed on him, not the enemy. Warfare never needs to be the focus. Handle your house but think about Jesus.

Your Little Kingdom

UpperDog handles his house. He neither ignores, denies, avoids or gets aggressive toward warfare. He simply tends to things like a man informed of the spiritual realm, but with no more drama or intensity than handling his laundry. His intensity belongs to the Lord. The enemy doesn't deserve it. UpperDog understands that while the enemy is defeated, our dominion still needs to be asserted. He surveys his kingdom and owns it actively. When he buys a new home, for instance, he attends to it spiritually as well as physically. Before moving in, he gathers his family together and they pray over the home and the land. They repent of and remove any enemy right or influence. They dedicate it to the Lord and his purposes. They ask that his blessing would fall over their new home and that his will would be done there as it is in heaven. He does this over all his spaces—home, office, cars, hotel rooms, etc.

If he buys a product that he thinks may carry a measure of enemy influence, such as essential oils or medications or some form of media, for example, he takes a moment to redeem it. He takes authority over the object, clears off all enemy right or effect, dedicates it to

God, blesses it and thanks his heavenly father for what is his in everything.

When he or one of his family goes to an unbelieving practitioner of any kind, he places the armor of God over them, blocks any authority of the practitioner's from establishing over them and prays that his influence would be by far the strongest in the room. He invites the Holy Spirit to use him to influence the practitioner. He thanks God for what he has planned and walks in with confidence.

When his daughter leaves for college, or his wife starts a new job, or he embarks on a journey, he pauses to come before the Lord. He takes authority over the issue. He takes apart any rights or attempts of the enemy to come against things in Jesus' name. He blesses the endeavor, dedicates it to God, thanks him for the pivotal moments in life and invites the Holy Spirit to reign actively in the enterprise. He's not pretending that warfare isn't real. He isn't obsessing about it either. He's just handling his house.

Blind Spot

I had the privilege of interceding for the men's retreat a couple of years ago. One morning while everyone was at breakfast, I went alone into the meeting room. I knew they were about to have a convicting discussion on letting go of pretenses and being genuine. I started my intercession by doing something we do at our Splankna trainings. On Friday morning before the conference starts, we walk around the room and lay hands on each chair. We pray for the person who will sit in that chair. We pray whatever God brings to mind, knowing that he has full knowledge of who will end up in that seat.

As I walked around the men's meeting room praying for each individual, God brought specifics to mind. I felt God's love and yearning for each of them and his desire for healing. I felt the sense of importance that these men have in the Kingdom. He made me realize the impact their wholeness would have in their families, in the church and ultimately in the big story.

I asked God what I could pray that would have the greatest impact. I felt the fire of the Holy Spirit in my hands. He showed me to pray specifically that when the moment of revelation and repentance came, the enemy had to leave. Specifically, that when each man became convicted and genuinely wanted to give up their form of inauthenticity, the enemy would be required to flee, having to completely leave in an instant in response to their repentance. God was giving me the grace to remove the warfare from all these men as soon as they repented. I felt like my three year old when she realized she could get rid of monsters by saying, "In Jesus name leave." I looked to heaven with excitement and reverence and said, "I can do that?"

Because the men no longer agreed with the enemy, his emissaries need not remain an influence in their lives. God revealed to me that at times the enemy would stay and tempt a person into an old pattern. Instead of departing completely, they hover and wait for an open door, an opportunity. God showed me that it is his intention that when someone repents they are set free. Basically, I'm only praying that it be the way God always intended.

I'm not sure if the entities of the enemy stay after repentance because they are not specifically cast out, or if they stay because of guilt. Sometimes believers on the passive side of things don't always understand the battle or how to fight it. What I knew for sure was the importance for me to pray in this particular way. I knew that it would lead to a deeper freedom for these men, liberation from the temptation. Because these men did not have a warfare worldview, they missed the house-cleaning piece. God allowed me to establish the cleaning as an automatic response to repentance.

It was like the enemy was staying just out of sight... in their blind spot. The blind spot being either denial of the spiritual realm, their own authority, or the sin itself. I knew God was planning to bring their sin into the light and they would have an opportunity to pursue freedom. I was simply joining them in their battle. Because of the legal rights involved, I could not just cast out something that these men were allowing of their own free will. What I was doing in that moment was partnering with the authority of Jesus. I was coming alongside my brothers in the spiritual realm and fighting with them in their blind spot.

Filter Example

I came home one night after a meeting to find that my son wasn't feeling well. He was complaining about his abdomen and was doubled over in pain. I started asking him questions. "When did it start? What were you doing?" etc. I discovered when the pain began. He had been reading a book to his brother, like they do every night. I asked him to bring me the book he was reading so I could look it over. There were no red flags, no reason to suspect the book would bring on this pain. Yet I had a feeling that something was up, so together we began to pray.

As we were praying, I felt led to break any curses coming through the book or the author. I bound all the warfare attached to the book and blessed both book and author. I removed all the effects it might have had on Ethan by the authority of Jesus and blessed him as well. After we concluded, Ethan felt better. The pain had subsided completely. He asked if he could finish reading the book. I proposed that we both pray about it and talk the next day.

By the next day it felt clear to me that finishing the book would no longer be a problem for Ethan now that we had prayed over it. I sensed confirmation from the Holy Spirit. We asked the Holy Spirit to place a filter over Ethan's mind so that as he read the rest of the book, any warfare or deception attached would be filtered out and only what the Lord wanted for Ethan would sink into his mind. We decided together that it would be our common practice from then on to always ask the Holy Spirit to place a filter like this over his mind when he begins a new book. Now Ethan has a new tool at his disposal. He has learned about standing in simple authority over the influences that come into his mind and submitting them to the Holy Spirit. We learned a valuable lesson through that experience. Please don't hear me saying that every book is ushering demons into your house. This is just an example.

That said, God has taught us that praying for a filter is quite useful any time you're going to be influenced by ideas, such as through a book, a speaker or an educational course. It's an example of how an UpperDog posture moves in authority amidst our culture. Whenever we teach a Splankna training we ask for the Spirit to place a filter over the minds and ears of the attendees, along with asking God to speak through us. We're well aware that our judgment is faulty. We know that we could be teaching something that is inaccurate or misleading even though that is not our heart's intention. So we "lean not on our own understanding"[87] and trust the Spirit to account for that. We believe in simple faith that the Spirit of God wants us to walk in truth and be steered clear from deception. After all, he is the one who "leads us into all truth."[88] We believe that he takes us up on the filter invitation.

Whenever we read a book, Christian or not, we simply pray for a filter. We ask God to let only what is true and useful take root in our minds. At first this may seem like we are coming from the underdog approach or from paranoia. I contend that it is not paranoid, just precautionary. It's just smart. It's good housekeeping. We lock our door every night before bed, not because of paranoia, but because it's wise. We know that there is a chance someone will break in, even though it is not necessarily a pending threat. We lock the door to be preventative and to take charge over our domain. Walking the tightrope of dynamic tension—not ignoring but not obsessing either.

Awhile back I was concerned that a leader in my oldest son's life was teaching him some distorted theology. I expressed this concern to my son and he asked for clarification. I knew the leader had a conservative view of the Holy Spirit and I had heard from others in the group that he was making statements like, "Miracles ceased with the disciples," and "God only speaks through the word," etc. When I shared this with my son he said, "I've never heard him say any of that." "Well," I said with motherly sarcasm, "maybe that's because you're a teenage boy and you don't listen." He replied with a smirk, "Or maybe it's because you prayed for a filter over me, so I only hear what is true!"

Touché.

My husband Joe read the recent book, *Heaven Is For Real*.[89] It piqued his interest in the kind of heavenly experiences the author describes. He found another book at the library about a near-death experience. Unbeknownst to him, the second book was written by someone embracing a false religion. When he read this second book he was having trouble processing. He was getting confused about God and heaven. He was confused by how different this author's experience was of "heaven." If she experienced this unorthodox vision of Jesus, what does that mean for our beliefs?

During this same time I had a dream. It was very vivid. Joe and I were having a picnic on the back porch and there were lions roaming around just beyond the chain link fence. Although they were always there, they never bothered us. During our lunch I noticed that one of the lions was getting closer. I said to Joe, "We need to get inside right now." So we headed for the door. At least I thought we did. I turned around to see that Joe wasn't coming with me. He stayed there in our endangered picnic spot and was cleaning up. It was obvious that Joe was not taking this threat seriously.

I got upset and insisted that we get inside. When I turned back around, there was Joe bent over picking something up and a lion had his mouth open over Joe's throat. I yelled at the lion like he was a disobedient pet, "No!" He looked at me out of the corner of his eye and whimpered, as if to say, "What? I'm not going to hurt him. I'm just playing." I commanded the lion to leave. It reluctantly withdrew from Joe's neck and slowly walked away. Every few steps he would turn around and look at me, hoping I would change my mind and let him "play" with Joe. For the rest of the dream Joe continued to dismiss the threat around us.

When I woke up, I spent time in prayer asking God about the dream. I talked to Joe about it. We talked to friends who were strong in faith. Eventually it seemed clear that the lion represented the god of that false religion that Joe had brushed up against by reading this book. Joe had approached this book innocently. He was not aware that it represented significant demonic influence. He was unwittingly putting himself in harm's way—not only himself, but also our family.

We need to stay alert. Not afraid, just awake. We are less vulnerable when we understand our position in the Kingdom. Shortly after this I asked Joe if he would read, *I Give You Authority* by Charles Kraft. He was eager to protect the family and understand his authority as the spiritual head of our family. He began to read it right away. I was on a Splankna trip when he finished it. He called me and shared that reading the book brought up strong emotions. He realized how much he was missing out on the influential position God gave him.

Ever since Joe has embraced this position, those kinds of dreams have stopped. Also, now that he has more understanding of who he is, he can be curious without being vulnerable. We need to know the truth about God. We need to know the truth about who we are. We cannot ignore or dismiss the threat of the enemy. We need to be clear and strong in our authority. We need to be "wise as serpents" in order to be "innocent as doves."[90]

When we embrace our responsibility to reign with him over the enemy, we are partnering with him. We are disseminating the victory that Jesus accomplished over the enemy at the cross. UpperDog is demonstrating that accomplishment, speaking for it into the heavens.

Partnering In Creativity

"Your talent is God's gift to you.
What you do with it is your gift back to God."
– Leo Buscaglia

God knows the secret plan of the things he will
do for the world, using my hand.
~ Toyohiko Kagawa

They say that as he painted, his head torqued upward, he was following the inspiration of the Old Testament. Michelangelo is said to have read and re-read the Scriptures during those four years of arduous creativity and his accomplishment on the ceiling of the Sistine Chapel is unparalleled. Did you know that the very first reference to the Holy Spirit guiding an individual was also artistic? In Exodus 31 we are told that it was the Spirit of God who filled the artisans with the knowledge and skill to design the temple and its articles. When we create we partner with him. God is a big fan of beauty. He could have created things to be simply functional but he opted for gratuitous splendor. He made a sunset lovely and a vista breathtaking. He even made our own physical forms beautiful to each other! Every time we create anything beautiful we are partnering, we are representing a core aspect of his nature.

But we don't just create beauty with him. We create ideas, objects, plans and structures. When we employ our creative abilities we glorify him. We are the only part of his creation that *can* create and he is pleased by it. My friend Beata arranges flowers. Aaron writes music. Wendy cooks and Jon captures images. All are glorifying God. When you galvanize your creative capacity you are partnering. You are a contributor in this story, not an observer. The story needs what you were made to create.

Look Mom, No Hands

A group of kids from our youth group attended a week-long camp called Lead the Cause University. The purpose of the camp is to prepare young leaders. Subsequently, the church requested that they give a presentation for the congregation. Because of Isaac's gifting in art, he was tasked with a drawing. The main focus was Acts 1:8 "...you will receive power when the Holy Spirit comes on you; and you will be my witness in Jerusalem, in all Judea and Samaria and to the ends of the earth." Isaac decided to pray and let the Holy Spirit lead him in his drawing. His drawing was almost complete when he came to me in defeat. "Mom, I can't draw hands. I've tried several times and they just don't look right." We both found it rather odd since he draws hands all the time with no problem. After a minute of reflection I considered that maybe God didn't want him to draw hands. I proposed that he go back to prayer and ask God to reveal how to conclude the drawing. Later Isaac presented his completed drawing. God didn't want hands after all. God led him to use fire in place of hands. Of course! The fire of the Holy Spirit!

This was a significant confirmation of the first time Isaac actually heard from God. His yearning to hear led us to take action. Our small group decided to watch Mark Virkler's series, *"4 Keys To Hearing God's Voice."*[91]

During one practice time in the series, we were instructed to ask God a question and journal what we heard. Isaac kept praying and trying to hear from God. Every time he would attempt to quiet himself, he would hear a taunting voice telling him that he would never hear. He would cast out the enemy and start again. The same thing happened several times. On the way home, he shared his hindrance with us. I promised Isaac that when we got home, we would pray against the warfare and he would hear. He said, "Mom as soon as you said that, I heard 'what if you cast us all out and you still can't hear?'" My eyebrows went up and my husband and I exchanged a knowing look. At that moment, I felt a confirmation from the Holy Spirit that he would indeed hear. So I assured Isaac with confidence that he was going to hear and the enemy would not be allowed to interfere.

As we were praying to clear off the warfare, I pictured myself standing in front of Isaac with my arms spread wide, holding the warfare behind me. God was showing me that my authority as his parent was standing between him and the enemy's plans. Once I felt that Isaac was completely protected, I suggested that we start with a simple question. He asked God, "How do you see me?" I instantly heard God say that he loved Isaac more than he can imagine. I gave Isaac a few minutes and asked what he had heard. He sidestepped the question and stated, "I think I just heard something from my own mind, to make me feel better." I clarified to him that it doesn't work that way. Usually what we hear from our own mind comes with a condition. For instance we might hear "You are awesome, but you could be better if..." The way our minds operate is more works-oriented. We have to earn accolades. God answers us directly and in love. Even when he rebukes, he does it in love. Still unaware of what I had heard, Isaac hesitantly said, "Well, I think I heard God say that he loves me more than I can imagine." When I told Isaac that those were the exact words I heard, he lit up. His hesitations and doubts began to diminish. His spirit was renewed.

I suggested we ask an additional question. We inquired, "What do you want Isaac to do with his gift of art?" I visualized Isaac humbly standing before God. God appeared gigantic while Isaac was so slight. Isaac had his head bowed in reverence and was holding his gift high, presenting it before God as an offering. When I asked Isaac, he revealed what he had heard with expectation and searching, "He wants me to give it to him." When I told Isaac of my vision, he was ecstatic. I think he floated up the stairs to bed that night.

When Isaac completed this first drawing with the assistance of the Holy Spirit, he learned to partner with God through what he specifically had to contribute. He has learned to partner with the Holy Spirit through his artistic gifting. He will often draw at church, during the sermon. This is just one of his drawings; he has many more. His drawings inspire and encourage others.

The Big Pie

Creativity is connected to gifting. Whether your gifting is artistic or relational, functional or intellectual, its *expression* is creative. God plants gifting into each one of us and then waits with bated breath to see what we will do with it. One of the most common hang-ups we see in the body of Christ is paralysis around "calling" because of a misunderstanding of partnership. Christians are asking, "What's the call on my life?" "What does God have for me to do here?" They think they missed the memo. Surely God must have broken in at some point and told them the "right" career path or passionate endeavor they were "supposed to" take and they weren't listening. But I'm convinced that the call of God on one's life is not pre-scripted. It is not mapped out for you. This life is not a game show, "OH! Too bad… you were supposed to pick door number two." "Wait! Wait! What did I say!? Door number one? I meant two!"

God gives gifting and its expression has many options. Think of it like a big pie, representing all the possible arenas of life. Each one of us is designed, gifted to belong in one of those slices of pie. In that arena, you're like a fish in water. You think that way, you intuit there, you belong. Inside of that slice of the pie, your gifting has flow.

You can "get in the zone" there like you can't in other arenas. Not that you can't function and even be productive in other pie slices, they're just not your home base.

Uniquely You

Be who God created you to be. I know it sounds trite, but it's easier said than done. I had a client this week tell me that she's impulsive and everyone says it's a bad thing, a character flaw. "But what if it isn't a bad thing?" I wondered out loud. "What if it's your design? What if you're gutsier than the average person? What if what you're calling a weakness is a strength as well? What if God made you that way for a reason?"

When I was talking to her, the Holy Spirit brought the apostle Peter to mind. When Peter got out of the boat and walked on the water to Jesus, he was being impulsive. He saw what his Lord was doing and followed. Impulsiveness is no worse than being cautious. Everything, when taken to an extreme, can be a problem. Suppose God wants to use that thing in you that the world says is a flaw. Suppose he created you to be a little impulsive or pensive, bubbly or strict. Sure these things could lead to bad behavior, but they could also lead to unique, radical obedience, and the story needs more of that. What attributes are you trying to overcome? Ask God what he wants to do with those. Maybe it's part of your brokenness that he desires to heal, but maybe it's part of your specific creation that he desires to use. Think redemptively towards *yourself.*

I'm Not One Of Them

Growing up, they had me stand on tables and sing wherever we went. (Usually something from *The Sound Of Music.* Come on, it was the 70's) Singing is a great love in my family. By my freshman year in college I was writing music as well. When I first moved to Colorado I heard about the Christian Music Conference in Estes Park. Every year, Christian musicians, singers and songwriters gather to share their craft and to compete for record contracts, etc. I decided to go. I entered an original song in each category and did pretty well. But then something pivotal happened.

One night at about 2:00 am, I was sitting in the lobby of the little hotel in Estes with a group of about twelve strangers who were also attending the conference. We were just sharing stories and laughing into the wee hours. Then someone said something like, "You know how sometimes God wakes you up in the middle of the night and you just *have* to write?" "Yeah, yeah!" they all agreed. "Yes, and how sometimes you can't help yourself. The Spirit is just downloading music through you!" Everyone joined in a chorus of enthusiastic resonance (no pun intended).

And in that moment I realized something that would change my life.

I did NOT know what that was like. Yes, I had an aptitude for music, but I had never been woken up by the Lord and compelled to compose. I had never been taken over in musical dictation. I had no sense of passion or ambition to write music, only a casual enjoyment of it. "Wow," I thought to myself. "I am not one of these people. They all have this same design and I don't." I realized in that moment that if you put me in a lobby at 2:00 a.m. with other psychologists talking about their passion to see change in their clients or with other aspiring theologians pondering the great questions of life, I would be in on the "yeah, yeah"-ness. But not here. It was a defining moment for me. I knew from then on that I was designed to fit into the psych/theology slice of the pie. Those are my people. That's how I automatically think, move, react. That's where I'm passionate—the healing of the soul, the searching out of truth, the empowerment of the body of Christ. "Wow, who knew!" I literally picked up my things, walked out, got in my Honda and drove back home to Denver. I've never again wondered if music is the call on my life. You see, UpperDog knows something special about calling and creativity.

It is grounded in desire.

You Want To Do What?

What you want is no accident. It may sound too good to be true, but the calling on your life, the arena in which you belong and are meant to operate will sound like fun to you. It will sound like a great adventure, a privilege. My friend Paula is one of the greatest people on the planet. She and her husband David are raising their two boys in Pakistan. It is the call on their lives to dig their hands into the cultural morass that is South Asia and speak for Jesus. Now I've got to be honest. I would rather get a daily root canal than be a missionary in Pakistan. But to Paula, it's a kick and a half. There's nothing she'd rather be doing.

People often say to me something like, "How can you stand it? How can you sit with people's pain and brokenness day in and day out? I couldn't take it!" But to me it's fantastic. It's fascinating and meaningful, ever-challenging and deeply satisfying. And that's how it is with God. When he gives a calling, he supplies it with the necessary desire. He "gives you the desires of your heart."[92]

He also supplies it with the necessary provision and spiritual protection to pull it off. Within your slice of the pie, there is an availability, a nearness and a provision of the Spirit of God that is unique. It's literally tailored for you there. The right timing, the finances, the people you'll need along the way, the ideas, the opportunities, all of it. It's all there, connected to your calling, waiting in your pie slice.

Intimacy with God is greater there as well. The nearness of his voice, of prompting, of his own joy and motivation welling up within you; it's all sharper within your calling. When you are operating creatively within your purposed arena of life, the connection to him is far more palpable. You can taste the partnership.

"So how do I find my slice of the pie?" you ask. There are several excellent books written on this topic as well.[93] We won't reinvent this wheel either. We'll just discuss the basics that apply to an UpperDog posture: Expectation and Movement.

UpperDog has to expect to be called, and move on inclinations. So where do you start? Start with desire. The things you desire are not as universal as you think. Yes, everyone wants to "make a difference." But the *how* is specific. I remember a client telling me that she wanted to work in hospice. "That's not normal," I said. "And I mean that in the best way." It was clearly in line with the call on her life to go into hospice work because it's not a universal desire. Most people do not think about hospice work and say, "Yeah, that'd be a blast." But to her it sounded great. As in her case, the things you desire were planted in you. They are meant to produce a distinctive harvest. Your harvest.

So begin with desire. Ask yourself and the Lord, "What do I love? What do I want?" Write down what comes to mind. Ask for confirmation in the form of ideas and opportunities. And then expect them. When a conversation turns to your desires, or a door opens, or a dream confirms, listen.

And then move.

When an idea comes to mind and you think it might be a confirmation, a leading of the Lord into an area of calling, move your muscles. Do

147

something, even if it's small, that heads in that direction. Maybe it's a phone call or a bit of research. Move and expect again. If you're hearing well, picking up on what he's putting down, then the next idea/opportunity will present itself in response to your first move. It's a collaborative dance. He moves, you move, he moves again.

If you move on an inclination and you're off base, the doors will close. Whether literally, like a rejection letter, or in a simple deflation of interest or passion. In that circumstance, move on another inclination. He is dying to collaborate. He does not need coaxing. He is not reluctant. Try him. The main difference between the Christian who enjoys the adventure of calling and the one who misses out is expectation and movement.

When I was starting out in my career, I knew what I wanted (I thought). The best thing I could think of within the world of Christian counseling was to work with one of the established national group practices like Samaritan or Minerth-Meier. But when I landed those jobs, the Lord would close the door and open up opportunities for private practice. It took me a while but I finally stopped throwing a fit and paid attention. I moved on the open doors he was presenting. I signed a three-year lease on an office space and a one-year monthly advertising contract all without a single client to bring me an income. I put the onus on God. "Well, this seems to be the direction you're offering, so it's on you if I starve." I dedicated my life direction to him and asked for his partnership. I moved on the open door and he blessed it. I never starved for the risk. Fancy that.

While the best thing I could come up with was to come under a well-established Christian psychology umbrella, God saw an even sweeter dream and I've been intensely grateful. But I never would've found it without expectation and movement. I had to expect that what was happening around me was a signal of his involvement. Then I had to move on it. But here's the important thing: that experience is not unique. I am not special. That very same interactive collaboration is being offered to you right now. It always has been.

Training

On the one hand, God repeatedly chooses the "least of these" to fulfill his grand purposes. He chooses David, the smallest and youngest. He chooses Bethlehem and Nazareth, the embarrassing little towns, no more than a wide spot in the road. He chooses Moses, the outcast, illegitimate criminal who doesn't speak well. But then on the other hand he says that the man of God needs to "be competent and equipped for every good work,"[94] and the Psalms uphold good training. "Do you see a man who is skilled in his work?" Solomon asks in Proverbs. "He will stand before kings."[95] Even though God finds pleasure in displaying his glory in our weakness, he also values training and skill. A good education is like fertile soil. God can grow a stronger crop where the nutrients are rich. Don't think that because he is willing to honor the untrained and uneducated that you are excused from the effort of becoming equipped.

The issue with training is much like the issue with money. Having money is not a problem. It is an opportunity before the Lord. The problem begins when we rely on our money, when we trust in it. The same is true for education and training. To be trained is to be responsible. Excellence honors God. We are his instruments. The better we are tuned, the more beautiful the music. The problem lies in our tendency to place our personal worth in our abilities or our degrees. Do you see that familiar dynamic tension? Be skilled and don't be defined by it. Be as equipped as you can be and then drop it all behind you and come before him with open hands.

Partnering In Obedience

The more we depend on God,
the more dependable we find he is.
-Cliff Richard

Everything we do that aligns with God's general will is an act of partnership, even if it's accidental as with the unbeliever. Every act of love, generosity, forgiveness, bravery, beauty or wisdom honors God. It does not take a supernatural encounter to partner daily with God in his overall will. He has given us so many descriptions of obedient behavior. We are never at a loss for "how" to obey him. Every moment is pregnant with obedient potential. Every human interaction has room for kindness or love. Every choice has the potential for goodness. The edge that UpperDog has in general obedience is that he has moved beyond sin management. He does not see obedience centrally in terms of sin,

but in terms of *contribution*.

He looks at his day and sees all the potential for life, for glorious expression rather than focusing on the potential for sin. He knows that sin management is the "milk" of the issue and he's focused on the "meat."[96] When his head hits the pillow he isn't thinking about all he did wrong that day or even of all the sin he avoided. He's thinking of what he contributed, what he added to the story through every selfless deed and brave decision.

Beginning in 1787, and lasting almost forty-six years, William Wilberforce fought single-handedly for the abolition of slavery in Britain.[97] God placed a passion in his heart that he could not escape. Weathering violent opposition both politically and personally, he stayed the course until the task was finally accomplished only three days before his death. This was a man who not only recognized that his passion was from God, but acted on it relentlessly. He did not need a divine sticky note to know that God was against the savagery that was exhibited in Britain's slave trade. He threw himself into what he knew was the heart of God and changed history.

And then there's specific obedience.

Of course we have some great examples of specific obedience in the Scriptures. But without realizing it, we tend to read these stories like colorful fiction instead of gritty reality. Logically we know they are real life accounts, but when we fail to see these people as *people* we tend to downplay the punch of their drastic obedience. I'm asking you to humanize these individuals in the midst of their well-known stories.

What might it have been like to hear Creator God tell you to build a gigantic boat in preparation for the coming rain that would destroy the earth? Not exactly your average walk to the sheep pen. When Noah made the decision to obey God in such a fantastic venture, his human spirit must have been full of fears. He must have weighed the pros and cons. The Scripture says he was the only righteous person, so maybe there was no hesitation. But that doesn't mean there were no emotions. Noah was a man. It may never have rained before, but he believed that God would flood the earth, so he obeyed and did something astonishing and unprecedented. He did what was ludicrous in the eyes of his contemporaries.

Then there's Abraham who picked up tents and camels, women and children and headed into the wild blue yonder, even though he had no idea where he was going. He left the comfort of his home, the only place he had ever belonged, to find a foreign land. We're familiar with that account, but this is what we miss: Abraham was just a regular guy. He had emotions. He had to swallow his pride and his fear and believe that God's plan was best. Later, God made good on a long-awaited promise and gave him a son, but then asked him to sacrifice that spectacular provision, and still Abraham obeyed. He reasoned that God had always been faithful to him, that God was bigger than death. If God asked him to sacrifice his son, it's because God can raise the dead. Imagine the distress that Abraham must have felt as he approached the place of sacrifice. Imagine the distress *Isaac* must have felt as his father prepared him for sacrifice. Abraham trusted beyond his human understanding and radically obeyed God's specific direction.

A convicted murderer, deserter and failure, Moses traveled back to Egypt and went toe to toe with Pharaoh because he was given specific orders. He obeyed God even when the people refused to believe that he was the deliverer. He fought for a people who didn't support him, possibly even reviled him. I wonder what we would discover if Moses kept a journal of his feelings and thoughts. Would we see some insecurity, doubt and questioning? Certainly. But he obeyed God, even when it was a lonely journey, and the people were not behind him. Ultimately he had to trust that God was faithful, even if no one else was.

Naaman obeyed humiliating instructions to dip seven times in the dirty Jordon River. Joseph trusted and obeyed when he was told that Mary was to bear the savior. Peter obeyed the outrageous edict to bring the Gospel of salvation to the Gentiles. We have many examples of the disciples obeying when they were instructed to flee, to preach and to go to places where they would be imprisoned.

I have noticed something over the years. When I obey the Spirit, there is a sense of rightness, even when people don't agree, criticize, or think I'm crazy. There is an indescribable peace that wells up inside of us when we are moving in the will of God. If you haven't experienced this, you may be spending too much time in the safe zone, where you obey the Spirit only when it's comfortable. But when you obey with risk, when you do the crazy thing, you feel like you can explode with sparks of the Holy Spirit. It doesn't matter who thinks you're nuts. It doesn't matter who is looking down on you. The satisfaction of knowing that you did what God asked is so rewarding that the consequences in this world are miniscule by comparison.

Joan of Arc is a great extra-biblical example of being willing to step out of the safe zone. She is remembered for having said, "I must be at the King's side...there will be no help (for the kingdom) if not from me. Although I would rather have remained spinning [wool] at my mother's side...yet must I go and must I do this thing, for my Lord wills that I do so."[98] At the age of 13, Joan had her first vision while she was in her father's garden. Three figures appeared to her and told her to assist the king and drive out the English. At first the king's men turned her away, but she did not let that deter her from following the instructions of the Lord. She continued going until she was able to join the king and history was made.

We read accounts like these and something natural in us says, "Yeah, but that was *MOSES*, that was *NOAH*. Of course *they* could be amazingly obedient. I'm just a regular Joe." But that's the irony. It was not their greatness and fame that enabled them such fierce, renowned obedience. It was their obedience that created their fame! They were regular people who simply obeyed. "Today if you hear his voice, do not harden your hearts."[99] If God says, "Go," move on it. You won't regret it.

Miss Tanya

I had noticed a growing tension within our ladies' Bible study. Miss Tanya was not my biggest fan. I didn't always go along with her opinions of how things should be done and she didn't appreciate it. It seemed that everyone else in the group went along with her for various reasons. Some were afraid to confront her, while others thought she was too fragile. I just tried to be cordial and friendly and let things roll off my back.

She had been hosting the study and wanted to take a break. The rest of the group, not realizing that she expected the *whole* group to take a break, decided to meet elsewhere. When she was ready to join again we allowed her to host because we knew it was important to her and we'd rather not upset her when we didn't have a preference. However, her resentment had grown during her sabbatical. Since I tend to be a strong personality she chose me to blame. However, rather than be direct, she decided to attack the whole group.

I felt a familiar heat rise up in me when her entitled rant began. Inside, I cried out to the Holy Spirit. I did not want my flesh to take over. I began praying, "Holy Spirit, lead me in this moment. Help me to say what you want me to say, nothing more and nothing less." When the rest of the room fell silent, God nudged me, "Speak up." So I did. I explained the inconsistencies in her outburst. I confronted her as clearly as I could. As we went back and forth, no one else spoke up even though I knew from other conversations that the other women were in agreement with me.

When I left that night and I was driving home alone, I cried out to God. "Why God? Why do you keep putting me in situations with these kinds of people? Why do I always have to be the scapegoat?" I vented with God because I knew that if I talked or vented to anyone else I would just be gossiping. I knew it wouldn't be productive and I wanted answers. This wasn't the first time he put me in a situation where someone turned against me because of what he led me to say. Being a peacemaker, similar to my husband, seemed like a much more appealing option. He has such a gentle, loving spirit. Why can't I just be a peacemaker?

For a couple of days I kept coming back to the feet of Jesus. I needed peace. Did I do what you wanted? Was it the Holy Spirit that led me or was it my own heart? I do have a hard time keeping quiet when something is unjust. Even as a small child I had to stand up to my gargantuan stepfather when he was abusing my siblings. I *had* to. I didn't care about the cost. In fact, I'd prefer he turn his angry eyes on me and let my siblings go.

This situation was no different. However, with this particular time I started to question myself. Finally I got my answers. A thought, a word from God crossed my mind. He said, "Did you say you would carry your cross?" Well, yes, and I'd say it again today, of course. He helped me to see that it wasn't about me. It was about Tanya. She needed to hear the things I said and he knew I would say them when no one else in her life was able or willing. He showed me that it doesn't matter if she's angry with me. Even if she hates me, she needed to hear those words. That is when peace came. That is when I realized that this is part of my gifting. I have a gifting and calling to speak the difficult truth, to say what others won't. I felt inspired. Basically I committed to God that I would anger anyone he wanted if it meant helping them. I do care about Tanya and I want her to be free of the bondage of entitlement and self-focus. If getting angry with me is what it takes, bring it on. Here I am, God.

The prophets of the Old Testament probably had some of the toughest assignments of all. They were regularly hated and even killed for their obedience in delivering God's messages to his people. But I promise you, from where they sit right now, there are no regrets. They aren't sitting amidst the great cloud of witnesses tonight wishing they had had a lesser task.

Learning To Listen

Remember how UpperDog is expectant? He expects to be called? Well, he also expects to be prompted. He assumes that Jesus sees him as he moves through his day. He assumes that Jesus is up to things all around him and would prefer to include him. So he interprets his experiences through an expectant lens. He pays attention.

In order to be active, meaningful partners with God, to be UpperDogs, we first have to be connected to him. Not just in a state of belief, but in relationship. In order to partner with him, I have to know what he's up to! Part of the aggressor's trouble is that they assume they do know God's will in a given circumstance. They miss that while God does desire many things generally that are in line with his character, he also actively *decides*. God is "working things to the good" in every individual moment. Yes he has a general will, but the enacting of his general will in this story involves a billion specific moments. It involves his *specific* will.

And his specific will is dynamic.

He's alive, active, in motion. He's working angles at every moment in the great tapestry. If I am to join God in that movement, what I need most is a clear line of communication. Scripture tells us that when we pray within his will, we can know that we have what we ask of Him. So in order to partner with him, we need to know what he would have us pray! I need to be able as Jesus said, to "see what the Father is doing."[100]

Learning to hear God, to pick up on his direction, his prompting, his subtle turns and grand schemes is critical in the quest for intimate partnership—the kind that moves closer to him than general obedience. In order to follow personal directions I have to learn to hear them. I can be the most skilled partner in the world, but if I don't know the task at hand, how can I participate? Listening is crucial for the UpperDog partner.

I Don't Hear God

My husband and I believe it's invaluable to spend one-on-one time with our children. It's always been a priority for us. When our oldest turned 13, it was my turn to have a weekend away with him. We went on a trip to southern Colorado and enjoyed hiking and hanging out in our hotel room. I knew in my heart that he and I needed to have a serious discussion about his faith and his walk with God. I explained to him that from my perspective it seemed like he wasn't really connecting with God, almost as if he was tagging along with the faith of his parents. He shrugged his shoulders and his expression was dispassionate. My heart stopped for a second.

When it comes to the command to "make disciples," my children are my most significant priority. My heart's desire is for them to know God and to love him with all their heart, mind, soul and strength. His nonchalant attitude really terrified me. We talked a little more and decided to take the issue to God in prayer and invite him to work on my son's heart through Splankna's emotional healing protocol. God revealed unbelief and shame in his heart. I asked him, "What comes to mind when you think about shame with God?" Immediately he broke down. His emotions became intense and I waited for him to gather himself. I couldn't imagine what this was about.

He looked at me with blurry eyes and said through sobs, "I've never heard from God." As he continued, he poured out his emotion. He was heartbroken over never hearing from God. But *my* heart took a leap. I was overjoyed. I know that sounds odd, but by his reaction I knew that deep within him there was a desire for relationship, and he yearned for God. I was optimistic.

"Remember when you woke up with a verse on your mind? We looked it up and it was just what you needed to hear. Honey, that *was* hearing from God!" I also reminded him, "Remember when you came home from school in fifth grade and asked if we could pray for the new girl who was struggling to catch on? That was God too! He was laying her on your heart." I saw a glimmer of hope in his eyes. He showed me a drawing he had sketched from a recent dream. He asked with anticipation and hope, "Could this be God speaking to me?" It undoubtedly was. We prayed about the inference within the drawing and God gave us some remarkable insight. He began to see the potential of a personal bond with God.

Like my son, many of us don't realize that we "hear" from God because we have a narrow understanding of his ways. Hebrews 3:15 says, "Today if you hear his voice, do not harden your hearts." This verse is assuming two important things: first, that you are likely to hear his voice today, and second, that you are likely to ignore it. God speaks dramatically and subtly and hearing him is a skill we develop. There are times when he breaks into circumstances and speaks audibly, supernaturally. But those are the exceptions.

Usually his workings with us are more quiet and personal. We need to understand that there are many different ways to hear from God, such as:

- The Bible
- Holy Spirit
  - Thoughts
  - Feeling/sense
  - Dream
  - Vision
  - Emotions
- Prophetic Words
- Prompting
- God's Audible Voice
- His Creation
- Supernatural Encounters

God is speaking. He has not withdrawn from his creation. He is still as involved and present as he's always been. We just aren't always tuned in. One of the most common discoveries of believers who learn to listen is that they were always hearing, they just didn't know it. God is currently speaking to you. As UpperDogs we have to know how to take direction, get the game plan downloaded and resound with the battle cry. Let's look at some of the ways we can hear from God.

The Bible

The Bible is our gift from the Father. It is often referred to as the "living word" of God. It is called the living word for a reason. The Bible seems to offer new insight each time we read it. How many times have you had this experience? You read a familiar passage and it speaks to you in a whole new way. You find yourself comprehending an idea as if it's the first time you've read it. The Bible is also the best way to test other modes of hearing from God. When you believe God is speaking to you in your thoughts, the Bible is a great resource for validation or redirection. If you hear something that is contrary to Scripture, you can be certain it's not of God. The Scriptures are also our measuring stick when a fellow believer offers us a word of prophecy. Check it with the Scriptures. We must remember that the Bible is our grounding wire. Listening to God should always trump listening to people. When you hear a sermon or a new teaching, ask God for his opinion. The Bible is an excellent way to ask God. Don't take someone's word for it.

You'd be amazed at how many "spiritual" phrases we use thinking they're Scriptures. "Everything happens for a reason"—not in the Bible! "God won't give you more than you can handle"—not in the Bible! "God helps those who help themselves"—not in the Bible! I'm not implying that our leaders and fellow believers are purposely misleading us. I'm just saying that we are all human. We are all learning and growing. In order for the Bible to be your standard upon which to gauge other ways of hearing, you need be immersed in it. A lazy mix of the words of Jesus and glib colloquialisms is not a useful measuring stick.

"The Word of God is living and active."[101] We're all so familiar with that statement that it can slip by unnoticed. But camp on it for a moment. The Bible is *living*? Really? What an incredible idea. We tend to come to the Scriptures as if they're old, dusty and well... dead. But the reality is that the Spirit of the Living God is contacting you when you read. He's reaching out of the words on the page and grabbing your heart and mind like a vice.

My kids are still young, so I'm lousy with cartoon metaphors. One of their favorites is *"Imaginarium."* In one of the episodes of this space-age-meets-heroes animation, the characters run into little aliens who attach themselves to the tops of their heads. When one of these playful creatures latches on, they compel their host to dance. These macho heroes are forced to jig and mambo their way across the planet whether they like it or not. I use that imagery in Bible reading and in prayer. (Seriously) When I come to the Word, I expect God to speak to me actively. I invite him to take an alien-like clamp onto my mind and move it where it needs to go. I do the same thing when I open session with a client. I ask God to take hold of my thoughts like a vice and turn them so I can think the things I need to think for this particular client. The Bible is alive. Invite it like a vice grip.

Show Me Scripture And Verse

It also needs to be mentioned here that while the Bible is living and active, God is bigger than the written word. There are Christians who believe that the Bible is the *only* way to hear from God. However, within the Bible's own pages we see many examples of God speaking to the disciples through other modalities. Although the disciples could refer to the Old Testament, they *wrote* the New Testament. The disciples heard from God through thoughts, visions, dreams etc. In the Gospel of John Jesus said, "The Counselor, the Holy Spirit, whom the Father will send in my name, will teach you all things and will remind you of everything I have said to you." This Scripture is very clear that God will communicate with us through the Holy Spirit. Still some will contend that the Bible was intended to be our only source of hearing from God. They believe that we are unable to communicate with God apart from the Bible. But the Scriptures themselves contradict this theory. Jesus is alive right now. He sees you right now. Why would he be mute?

Holy Spirit

Our church was going through a transitional period and some of us were meeting as advisors to the leadership. One of the leaders asked me if I would talk to the group about hearing from God. He asked if I could explain how it works. I was a little overwhelmed. I heard from God, yes, but I had no idea how to break it down into a formula. It felt like someone was asking me to explain how the electricity gets from the electric company into my house. I took the question to God. I was driving home from that meeting and brought the subject before God. "So God… how do I hear from you? How is it that I can hear from you when so many others struggle?" He said simply, "You expect to. You listen." Hmm. As I thought about that, I realized that it took me years to hear from God, to learn to *expect* to hear because I was not taught to expect it by those who brought me to faith. For several years I had been asking God questions, but in the beginning, I didn't really expect an answer.

I first learned to listen because I had a realization about prayer during a church retreat. Over Labor Day weekend our entire church went to the YMCA of the Rockies and spent the weekend learning from many teachers. During a class about prayer, I had a profound insight. It occurred to me that I didn't have to have a formal prayer time with God. I had always believed that I needed to spend a significant amount of time praying in the morning. I struggled with this because I'm not a morning person. I always felt like a bad Christian and a disappointment to God because I usually missed my morning appointment. When I realized that I could talk to God *anytime*, I felt a sense of freedom and excitement. It was one of those moments when you think, "How did I not realize this?" Imagine the freedom. I could talk to God all day long if I wanted to. He is omnipresent after all.

That is when I learned to dialog with God. I talked to him when I was driving, in the shower, while I was doing dishes. It felt like there was never a time when I wasn't talking to God. It's only natural when you are constantly connecting with God, you will eventually begin to recognize that he is answering you. In those early days, the first way I realized he was dialoging with me was in the fairly consistent stream of insight. At first I thought all those brilliant ideas were mine, but at some point along the journey I realized that I'm just not that clever. That was the beginning of listening to God. It took me years to recognize when God was speaking to me and of course I'm still unsure at times.

The first time it hit me that I had heard an answer from God was when I was in an accident on I-25 with an uninsured motorist. Fortunately, I had plenty of coverage. My neck and shoulder were injured and I required considerable care. Every time I moved my right shoulder there was a painful clicking. My scapula was actually jammed and cutting into my levator every time I moved my arm. After several months of chiropractic care and massage therapy, the clicking ceased and my arm wasn't fatiguing as quickly. My insurance company called to offer me a pain and suffering settlement. The agent on the phone offered me $1,500. "Is that acceptable?" she asked. I had no idea what to expect or how to respond. I asked her for time to pray and discuss it with my husband. Neither my husband nor I had any idea what was fair. I was talking to God about it, as I was accustomed to doing. I was in the shower enjoying the silence and I thought I heard God say, "Ask for $4,000." I laughed to myself. Did I just hear that? "Okay God," I said. I'll ask for $4,000." Why not, right? Then I realized something. $3,000 would cover my school loan and the other $1,000 was for him. My next words to God were something like, "So, I'm going to do this. I'm going to ask for $4,000. If this is from you it'll work out and if not I'll let it go. Although I have to admit, I don't think they'll agree. I'm asking for more than double what they offered. But, I know you are God and you can do anything."

Later that day the insurance agent called back and asked if I had considered their offer. I said, "Yes, and I don't think it's fair." She asked what I thought was fair. I told her, and then suddenly I started telling her why. I was shocked that I *knew* why. It was like I was on autopilot, like I was inspired. I explained my hourly wage, my loss of work from an injured shoulder and how much money I could have made if I was able to work—which coincidentally equaled $4,000. What? I was shocked by my own words. It reminded me of Jesus telling the disciples not to worry about what they will say, because the Holy Spirit will do the talking. God is awesome! After I (Holy Spirit) made my case there was a moment of silence and she said, "Hold on a second." I was speechless (I'm rarely speechless). I sat there marveling in amazement of what had just transpired. A few minutes later she came back on the phone and said without hesitation that my request sounded fair and she would mail me a check. My jaw might have actually hit the floor.

After I received the check, I paid off the school loans and asked God what I should do with his money. I didn't hear anything but I felt like he wanted me to hold on to it. For the next year or so I would randomly check in and see if God wanted me to give it yet. Finally one day I was sitting in church and our minister was talking about needing money for the Hurricane Katrina relief effort. Very clearly God said, "Now." I wrote the check at that moment and gave God's money back to him. (I love God!)

And God Said...

Occasionally God does speak audibly as well. I've only heard the audible voice of the Lord twice (so far). The first time I (Sarah) was asleep in the back of an 18-passenger van. There were about eight of us on our way back from a spring break campaign in Ft. Collins, Colorado. It was about 3:00 a.m. in early spring and the road was iced over. Several hours earlier our defroster had broken, so the guys in the front kept having to pull over every few miles and scrape the ice off of the windshield. So obviously the conditions were poor but it was a long flat stretch of highway with no one around and we were all more than ready to get back to campus and a warm bed, so we just kept trudging onward.

Like I said, I was asleep, stretched out on the back bench, when I was awoken by an audible voice saying, "Grab on. You're going over." Without even sitting up, I stretched my arms around the back of the bench in front of me and held on tightly as we began to slide. We rolled that van three full times before came to a crunching, frozen stop. Everyone in the car landed on the bench behind them and I would've been thrown out of those two mangled back doors if God hadn't spoken to me.

Four years later, it was about 6:30 in the morning and again the interstate was empty. I was finishing graduate school and I had taken a long, lonely road trip to check out a domestic missions opportunity in Indiana. I was heading back to Abilene with the sunrise streaming in through my driver's side window. Cruise control was set to 78 mph (I know, I know). I had Dennis Jernigan blaring, my seat reclined and my left leg draped up over the steering wheel. I was settling in for a long, quiet day.

Then suddenly I heard a voice coming from the passenger side of the car, as audible as if someone was sitting there next to me. "Your right front tire is about to blow." I was shocked. What on earth? I whipped my leg down off of the dashboard and grabbed on at 10 and 2. Within about two seconds of getting my bearings on the steering wheel, "POW!" my front tire exploded and I nearly lost control of the car. Twice, the voice of the Lord has saved my life. We share these stories as examples of how he does choose to speak to us in an audible voice at times, although it doesn't seem to be his venue of choice. He usually prefers the kind of subtlety that requires intimacy to recognize.

Three Sources In the Universe

The most common way I (Sarah) hear from God is in clear thoughts. Our human minds work in a dot-to-dot fashion. You can be lost in daydreaming and notice that you're thinking of something particularly random. If you stop and ask yourself, "Wow. How on earth did I get to that?" you can actually trace back your thought process. You can look back through those dots and see, "Oh yes, that thought led to that one, which led to that one…" etc. But when God moves in your thoughts it often feels separate from that linear pattern. I can be moving along in my dot-to-dot sequence, this thought leading to the next and then suddenly there's an idea that's discontinuous. I did not get there in my pattern. I didn't reason myself to that conclusion. It just appeared independently, all on its own, concise and resonating as true.

So I can hear you asking, "But how do you *know* if it's God?" You don't. Thus the dynamic tension. We'd rather it be that we hear audibly, supernaturally once or twice in a lifetime and otherwise we're off the hook. But that's not his style. That wouldn't develop intimacy. Outside of those miraculous audible moments, you won't know for certain much of the time. That's why it's a developed skill. Always hold loosely what you think you're "hearing" no matter your maturity in Christ. None of us are perfect hearers. Mark Virkler has a great study course on learning to hear God. That's a good resource to explore.[102] If you think you might be hearing from God in one of these ways we've discussed but you aren't sure, consider this:

There are only three sources in the universe:

1. *God*
2. *People*
3. *The enemy*

When you think of it that way, discernment is somewhat easier. Everything that crosses your mind has to come from one of those three sources. Pause your reading here and try something with me. Close the book for a moment and invite God. Invite him to say anything he would like to say to you. Be quiet just for a moment and notice what comes to mind.

(Go ahead, I'll wait.)

So, what did you hear? Slip it through our "three sources" grid. If you heard something in the "I love you" genre (by far the most common thing people hear in this exercise), ask yourself which of the three sources that's likely to come from. Is the enemy going to put the thought, "I love you," into your head? Certainly not. Are you likely to say that to yourself? Possibly, but not likely. Most of us are much rougher on ourselves than that. But is God likely to say that to you? Of course he is.

Let's try another easy one. Let's say you heard something in the realm of "You're stupid." Which of the three sources is that most likely coming from? Even if God was looking to correct you in some way, "You're stupid," is just not his style. All messages of condemnation, shame and threat come from the enemy. What if you heard something like, "I can't hear anything. I'm discouraged." Now that sounds like us, doesn't it?

When we practice hearing in our Splankna trainings, there is always a percentage of people who are putting heavy pressure on themselves. They are striving to hear. They are focused on their own "ability" to hear rather than on the character of God. Turn your attention away from yourself. Don't think about whether or not you are "good at hearing." Just think about it from God's perspective. He's the one who says he wants to communicate with us, to move in our minds and hearts. Lean on trusting in him; believe that he wants to speak. It's not an issue of your competence. It's an issue of his character.

One more caveat. Remember that God is multifaceted. He pours his loving words over us, yes, but he also has difficult things to say at times. God does not always whisper sweet nothings in your ear. I (Sarah) have struggled with food and weight for all of my adult life. It has been exasperating. One night I was having a fit with God about it. Particularly, I was making the case that he should've healed me of this problem because I represent him publicly. I was explaining to him that when I stand up in front of a crowd of people and share these wonderful tools for emotional healing, I'm a walking billboard of hypocrisy. I'm selling the healing tools of God while carrying forty extra pounds of emotional weight! "It's not like that," he said. "Oh no? I asked. "They think I look fine?" "No," he said. "They don't think of you at all."

Oh.
Right.

One evening, I (Heather) found a quiet place in the house. I wanted to be alone with God. I began by praising him for who he is. Then I asked him to give me a word. "Tell me anything you want," I said, "I just want to hear from you." And then I heard a word: "hypocrite." All of the sudden the word "hypocrite" was clear and sharp in my mind. I reasoned that there must be some enemy interference going on. Why would God give me such a negative word? Certainly God is more loving. I did a little warfare prayer and asked God to block all enemy contact. I went back to a surrendered posture with God and asked again for a word—anything you want God. And there it was. Very clearly the word "hypocrite" was on my mind again. I reasoned that either the enemy was really messing with me or God had something deeper to say about this word. "Okay, if this is you God, would you please explain?"

God lovingly showed me an area of my life where I had not been living according to my beliefs. I work so diligently with my clients, bringing everything to him. However, when it came to my own family, I had been neglecting their hearts. He had healing for them too and I wasn't pursuing it. He showed me that when it came to them, I would try to "fix it" instead of surrendering to him. I was cut to the heart and determined to change this pattern.

God, in his love, opened my eyes to an area of brokenness. He called me to a higher standard. The word might have been negative, but the message was pure love and concern for my heart and for the hearts of my family. Yes, most of the time God is a gusher. He loves to pour his adoring words into our hearts. But he is not one-dimensional, and neither is love. Real intimacy with him would have to include the occasional correction. Expect to hear him tell you of his affection for you. But if all you EVER hear are sweet nothings, compliments and invitations to go fishing, be suspicious.

Poor Hearing

When UpperDog gets the impression that the Spirit is inviting him to move, he moves. That's the kicker—he moves. That's how he gets better and better at discerning what is and what is not the prompting of God. Good old trial and error. When he moves on a suspected prompting and there is good fruit, he gains confidence. When the fruit is absent or contradictory, he learns from it and trusts that there is grace over it.

At Splankna our calendar year is September to September because our main promotional venue is the American Association of Christian Counselor's conference each year in Nashville. Our practice is to come before the Lord and ask him where he would like us to take the trainings over the next year. We listen and write down the cities that come to mind. We then pray over them for a few weeks, asking for further confirmation and we come back together and compare notes. We're well aware that what we hear can be coming from three different sources, like we just mentioned, so we hold things loosely.

One year during this process I heard "Toronto" as a city where we should take the training. We included it in our prayer list as usual and it made the cut. But as the weeks approached for the Toronto training date, there were no registrations. We asked God about that and waited. Still nothing. Eventually we cancelled that training and chalked it up to imperfect hearing. Sometimes that happens. Sometimes you will hear incorrectly. The sooner you get okay with that, the sooner you can engage.

As I was gazing upon my young son, I was in awe of God's handiwork. I didn't plan this little guy. In fact, I had decided that our family was complete with three kids. Sure I liked the name Levi and I had believed that God had a Levi for our family, but when my third baby was a girl, I figured I was wrong. I talked to my husband and reasoned that our family was wonderful and full of love. Maybe it's time to be done having kids, after all I had endured enough in three very tough pregnancies. Of course I believe in asking God for his will. "God, do you want us to have a fourth? Do you have a Levi for us?" We prayed for a few months and when God remained silent, we decided to be done. I figured this was one of the areas where God would bless us either way. I remember exactly what I prayed: "Well God, it seems that you are leaving this decision up to us and I'd rather not be sick for nine more months. We've decided to be done. Of course we want your will and not ours, so if you do have another one for this family we invite you to do your will." We proceeded with the vasectomy. Literally the next day we found out that we were pregnant with a fourth baby.

Regardless of our plan and prevention, God gave us Levi. I have never been more pleased that I prayed for God's will. As I stood there staring at this amazing gift from God, my heart was full of astonishment. God knew what I wanted and needed even when I had no idea. Levi was this marvelous little bundle of love. God knew the world needed him and therefore created him. Every time he lights up a room with his loving nature, I am reminded of how great God is. Sure I felt great love and gratitude for the first three, but this was different somehow. I guess with the other three I felt like they were more my will. We wanted them, we planned them and we had them. With Levi I recognized that I didn't know I wanted him, I didn't plan him and yet in God's greatness he showed me that he knows me better than I know myself. I laid the options out before the Lord, asked for his will and then moved on what I thought he was saying. Even when we don't hear correctly, he is still able to redirect us. In the adventure with God, you've got to come to peace with the fact that you will get it wrong sometimes and that he has more than enough grace to cover that. You keep engaging even though you won't always produce good fruit.

Because there will also be times when the fruit is wonderful…

Do What?

Hearing from God when you ask a question is amazing. But how about when you didn't ask? What happens when God prompts you to action? On occasion we dismiss those callings because they are uncomfortable. We justify, "That probably wasn't God." We talk ourselves out of those awkward promptings to avoid being uncomfortable.

In order to avoid distractions, I spent a lot of time at Chick-fil-A during the writing of this book. (Sarah and I laugh because many of my stories start with "So I was at Chick-fil-A the other day and…") Well, one day *when I was at Chick-fil-A* ☺ God brought one of the employees there to my heart and mind. He impressed a longing on me to pray with her. It was a little awkward. She was sitting and talking with the restaurant owner. I had to find the courage to walk to their table, wait for them to acknowledge me, and then ask if I could pray with her. God doesn't seem to concern himself with our comfort. It reminds me of times when I was a child and I heard an adult say, "See, that wasn't as bad as you thought," when beforehand you thought you might die if you followed through with whatever they were suggesting.

Several years ago, I was minding my own business when out of the blue God prompted me. I was sitting in on a church meeting when the Holy Spirit brought someone to mind, a person I had met only a few times in a committee gathering. I had met with Rick and another pastor a few times to plan a "More Than Conquerors" weekend event. At the event I met Rick's wife, Carrie. It was such a brief encounter that I didn't remember her name, only that she wasn't feeling well that weekend. I couldn't concentrate on the meeting because I kept feeling an urging from the Holy Spirit. It appeared that God wanted me to reconnect with Rick and Carrie.

At first, I thought, "Maybe this is my own thought. Maybe God isn't calling me. Maybe I'm trying to get involved in something for my own motives," (although I had no idea what those motives might be.) The lack of my own motive should have been the first clue that it wasn't coming from me. My prayer at that moment was, "God, I'm not sure if this is you prompting me or if this is just my own thought. I'm going to go distract myself and forget about this. I trust you God. If this is from you, you will bring it back tomorrow."

Well sure enough, I got home and lost myself in a Francine Rivers book and forgot, until the next day when I was going about my normal routine of talking to God and Wham! Rick and Carrie were on my heart. Again, I felt the deep urgency of the Spirit. I knew God was definitely prompting me. I emailed Rick and asked if his family could come for dinner. He replied, "Sure, we're free in two weeks." I smiled at God with uncertainty, with no idea what to expect. I prayed, "Okay God, two weeks to tell me why I'm having them over." I was filled with peace, as if he smiled and said, "You'll know."

When this amazing family came for dinner, we were all instant friends. It took only a short time and I knew what God was up to. I was asking questions about them and at the same time having an unspoken conversation with God. Carrie told us that she had been suffering from debilitating fibromyalgia for the last five years. She shared how she had tried everything from traditional medicine to deliverance ministry. As we moved through the conversation Rick mentioned that he was a licensed therapist as well as a minister. Rick also said that he had no intention of ever being in private practice again. He was frustrated with managing symptoms and seeing little change in clients.

It felt like God was smiling. I kept looking to him with a grin in my heart thinking, "Seriously God?" The Holy Spirit was revealing to me that God was going to heal Carrie of her fibromyalgia. He also showed me that he had plans for Rick to learn Splankna Therapy. They asked Joe and me about our lives and we talked about our respective jobs. They seemed intrigued with Splankna. As the night was closing, I was pretty fired up by the Holy Spirit, not really caring if I sounded crazy (and I knew I did). I said, "So guys, I have to be honest with you. I had you over to get to know you better. But there is another reason. I also felt called by God." I said to Carrie, "I think God wants to heal you of the fibromyalgia and I think he's going to use Splankna to do it. What do you say? Want to give it a try?" She agreed. I decided not to share with Rick what the Holy Spirit had revealed about him. I thought it would be more impactful for God to show him personally.

Only three sessions later, Carrie was reporting that the fibromyalgia pain was gone. Her energy had returned, and she was able to do things for herself. Praise God! Shortly after beginning with Carrie, Rick came to see me. He wanted to see what this Splankna Therapy thing was all about. I recall he said, "I have my wife back and I want to know what you did to make that happen." After his session, he said with certainty, "I have to learn this!" I smiled and said, "I know you do!" They *both* attended our next Denver training. God hadn't revealed his entire plan to me. He was going to use both Rick and Carrie as his healers.

After working with them, I noticed a ripple effect. They referred a local client to me, who referred a client from New Mexico, who referred a client from Texas. Becca came from Texas with overwhelming depression. This educated and usually articulate woman was barely able to form a sentence. She had experienced a deep emotional break a year prior. Her entire life was suffering. Over the course of our first intensive, three days, God brought dramatic healing for her. True to his nature, he filled my heart with his love for her. She made the trip to Denver several times throughout her healing process. One day as she and I were praying, we asked God a question and listened. I heard God clearly say, "I did it all for her." He was enlightening me that back when he called me to work with Carrie, his plans were infinitely larger than I realized. He knew the work with Carrie would lead to Becca.

I realized how profound and fathomless are the plans of God. There is no possible way we can comprehend what God is orchestrating. As I was pondering all of this, God continued. He said, "And I did it all for Carrie, and all for Rick, and all for Cynthia, and all for Jana." Talk about mind blowing. I began to see that I don't know anything! Even when we think we understand, God's cleverness and knowledge is inconceivable to us. Inconceivable! (I do not think that means what you think it means.) We cannot comprehend his immeasurable love. It's beyond our grasp. His mind works in ways ours cannot even appreciate. His plans are for the multitude and yet for each individual at the same time. He was revealing to me that in his own unique way, it was all about Becca while it was also all about Carrie. I would soon discover that it was all about me too.

I remember as I was sitting back and watching what God was doing I was astonished. I certainly recognized my desire to always follow the treasured lead of the Holy Spirit. Communication with God is essential! In John 16, Jesus said, "It is for your good that I am going away. Unless I go away, the Counselor will not come to you. But if I go, I will send him to you. When he, the Spirit of truth comes, he will guide you into all truth. He will speak only what he hears from God, and he will tell you what is yet to come."[103]

A Boy And A Bus

We were stuck at the Chicago airport waiting for our flight. There was nothing much to do so I glanced at the television screen overhead. The news caught my attention. Even though I'm not typically a follower of the news, this particular story intrigued me. I later realized it was the Holy Spirit prompting me, "Pay attention." A disturbed man had murdered a bus driver, taken a five year old boy and was holding him hostage. I distinctly recall shaking my head and thinking, "This is why I don't like the news." For me the news can be a life-sucking, negative abyss.

However, once I started to watch, I was engrossed and surprisingly not feeling hopeless. They stated that the kidnapper was a veteran who may be suffering from PTSD or some kind of delusion. It certainly appeared that the kidnapper was dealing with inner demons as well. As we have discussed, we are living in a legal universe. The man's demonic attachments can only do what is allowed. In some way, he is letting them stay and influence his life and behavior. I asked God, "What can I do to help this boy?" I had the most clear yet peculiar idea. I knew what to do and how to pray. I also felt a familiar earnestness and determination from the Holy Spirit.

He led me to pray that whenever the man was in the boy's presence, all of his demons were to be frozen and unable to operate, that nothing demonic was allowed to touch the boy or influence the kidnapper toward him. They may have legal rights to the kidnapper but they had no right to the boy. Even as I write this, I feel the fierceness of that truth in my spirit. I asked God to assign angels all around the boy to protect him. It was such an amazing revelation, and yet it seemed so obvious. I felt like God was giving me the authority to remove those demons because they had no right to the boy and they had to back off. So I interceded with confidence.

About a week later I was in a session and my client asked me if I had heard about the case. I realized that I hadn't even thought about it since the day I prayed. "What happened?" I asked. My client told me that the boy was rescued and seemed to have suffered no harm. The moment she told me that, I felt the Holy Spirit's energy wash through my whole body. God said, "See what we did?" I was overcome with joy and possibility! I was in awe of what God allowed me to do with him and I began to wonder what the future held. I'm not exceptional in any way that was helpful in that situation. My only attribute in the moment was that I heard and I obeyed.

It was like God was saying, "I need your help. Fight for this boy." God wanted someone *here* to partner with him, to stand up and be this boy's advocate, to combat the enemy and remind him of the law. Someone who was willing to ask him, "What does that look like?" More than just a cry-of-the-heart prayer, a partnering prayer! Had that been my boy, I don't know if I would have had a clear enough mind to listen and be led. Isn't God wonderful, that he created us for community, where we can fight for each other? Do you remember the battle the Israelites fought against the Amalekites in Exodus 17? As long as Moses held his arms up the Israelites were winning. When he got too weak and was unable to hold his arms up, Aaron and Hur held them up for him. We also have many opportunities to stand with our team and win the battles, to hold up each other's arms, especially against the enemy where the battle has already been won.

God made it clear that it's not my calling to watch the news and pray and fight for every case (in my excitement I considered that). I know that when he desires me to, he will bring it to mind. This is another dynamic tension: that on the one hand I'm expected to move, to cooperate with God, but on the other hand I can't heal/minister to everyone. Even Jesus didn't. I have to learn the skill of navigating what is and isn't given to *me* to do. "I only have to do what I can find," Amy sings.[104]

Just Orange

God is interacting with us constantly. He can't help it. He's everywhere animating everything! So much of the time "hearing" is just noticing one's own sensations and being willing to consider that things might be from God. For instance, God can speak to you through a clear thought, a physical sensation, a "random" imagination, an unexplained emotion, etc.

In our Advanced Training conferences for Splankna we begin with a simple exercise. The attendees get into groups of three and we practice listening to God. (As a rule of thumb, it's much easier to develop your listening skills when you're employed on behalf of another. Our objectivity is so poor when we're in prayer for ourselves that our hearing is clouded.) Each triad decides who will go first and the other two simply lay hands on them and invite God. We coach them to turn off their censors and ask God what he has for this person. The challenge is to notice without over-rationalization—to offer whatever comes no matter how irrelevant it may seem.

One weekend, someone did a great job of the whole "don't censor" injunction and told the person she was praying for that when she invited God to speak on her behalf, she saw the color orange in her mind.

Just orange.

Now how many of us would've had the courage to offer "orange" to a stranger in prayer? It would be so natural to discount that impression, wouldn't it? But when the prayer recipient heard it, she broke down in tears. Orange was the color she was painting the nursery for her expected newborn that she had just lost in a painful miscarriage. She felt God's intimate acknowledgement of her pain. Of course it could have been that orange was not from God, that it was from her own mind. But she took a risk, and it was through that risk that she took a step forward in her listening skills. She pumped a little listening iron.

Four-Leaf Clover

A pastor in Texas tells this story:

"I have a close friend named Jason who felt like God was telling him something completely random. To act on what he thought God was saying would potentially be a form of social suicide. He heard the faintest whisper: "Find a four-leaf clover and give it to that girl over there." If you've never looked for one, four-leaf clovers are as easy to find as W.M.D.'s in Iraq. Jason looked and then gave up, assuming that the "whisper" in his spirit could not possibly have been God. But it persisted. He returned, and after a long search found the evasive lucky charm. That was actually the easy part. The hard part was walking up to a total stranger—a teenage girl, prone to thinking he was creepy—and then convincing her that he had a message from God about a mutated weed. "I know this is completely random," he said, "but I felt like God wanted me to give you this four-leaf clover." He must have closed his eyes waiting for her to point at him and laugh. Instead, she burst into tears saying, "My boyfriend and I just broke up and I've been so sad about it. I felt like God didn't care about me, so I said, 'God, please show me that you do care about me. If you give me a four-leaf clover then I'll know you still care about me.'"[105]

Really God? A four-leaf clover? That feels about as legitimate as hearing "tooth fairy." But this guy moved. He obeyed in spite of uncertainty. He was willing to look foolish and his risk paid off. You rarely know with absolute certainty that a prompting is the voice of the Lord considering the influence of our own thoughts and the enemy, but you can only sharpen hearing through movement.

Charcoal And Indiana Jones

One of our Splankna Practitioners tells the story of being in a first session with an unbelieving client. She had asked the Lord to use her in any way he wanted in order to bring not only healing to her new client, but the Gospel itself. In the middle of conversation on an entirely different topic, she heard the clear words, "charcoal drawings." Odd. She brushed it off and re-engaged the conversation. Then it came again, "charcoal drawings." She had just been through our Advanced training and had just finished practicing hearing. It was fresh on her mind that she should take a risk and offer something even if it seems wild. So she did. "I have to tell you something," she said sheepishly. "As we've been talking, the Lord has said something to me twice now. 'Charcoal drawings.' Does that mean anything to you?"

Well, you can guess what happened. This woman was a passionate and talented artist and charcoal was her main medium. The practitioner was not aware of that, but the Lord was. In that moment, the client was stunned. The practitioner could have given an informative speech on the existence of God. She could have waxed eloquently on his characteristics, but none of that would've convinced that client of his immanent reality more than "charcoal drawings."

Developing your listening skills will require risk. God is a big fan of risk. He's famous for rewarding it. You have to *move* on something you think might be from him. It's the movement that tests it. Little by little, if you will move on these promptings, you will grow in ability to discern what is and is not from God.

I love the visual depiction of this idea in the third "Indiana Jones" movie. Do you remember it? Indie has been hopping along on his wild, cryptic adventure when suddenly he comes to a stop at the precipice of a cavernous drop-off. His instructions say that he must walk to the other side but there is no bridge, only a seemingly endless compilation of rocky spires rising up from below, just waiting to impale him. He is at a crossroads. There is no apparent way to get to the other side, but if he stays put, his father will die. So he does the astonishing thing. He takes a step out into nothing, over an endless cavern, trusting blindly that his instructions are trustworthy even though his senses say otherwise. And to his amazement (and ours) his foot lands on something solid!

As he balances, he gazes down once more and realizes, only from this vantage point, that there is an optical illusion in place. Only after taking an initial step does it become clear that there actually are steps across the cavern but they cannot be discerned from the safety of the edge. Once he realizes this he flies swiftly, stone to invisible stone, to the safety of the other side.

And such is life with God.
Only in our movement do our steps appear before us.
To partner you must hear.
To hear you must move.

Partnering In Prayer

*"Most of us wait until we're in trouble, and
then we pray like the dickens.
Wonder what would happen if, some morning, we'd wake up and say,
'Anything I can do for **you** today, Lord?'"*
~ Burton Hillis

There are many kinds of prayer. The first kind we usually learn is what John Eldredge coined the "cry of the heart" prayer.[106] This is when we're gushing out our insides before God. Whether it's gratefulness, pain, fear or anger, this is our cherished "connection prayer." This is just laying ourselves out before him in intimacy. This comprises by far the biggest chunk of our prayer lives and rightfully so. Unfortunately though, most Christians never progress past this point. They never venture into partnering prayer—UpperDog prayer.

Partnering prayer includes warfare prayer, prayers of blessing and authority, and *contributing* prayer. Prayers for healing, for miracles, for provision. Prayer to stop the rain. Or as we call it at the Splankna Institute, "Creative Prayer."

Creative prayer is the kind that's meant to get things done. It is grounded in intimacy already enjoyed and warfare handled. It is productive. Passive theology, as we've already established, would logically stop at intimate prayer. The cry of our hearts would be all we have to offer God if we are mere observers in the story. But Scripture paints a different picture. UpperDog wants to be as involved as possible with the Hero. He knows that as John Wesley said, "Prayer is where the action is." So he nurtures his relationship with God, handles his house, and then asks,

"So? What are we doing today?"

Variables

As we discussed in Chapter 7, underdog Christian, if he errs on that passive side of things, thinks that when he prays he is coaxing a reluctant God into action. Subsequently he asks and waits. If nothing appears to happen, he reasons that God did not agree with his petition. He asked the wrong thing, or God failed. Adversely, aggressive underdog thinks that if he prays and nothing happens, *he* failed. He just didn't believe hard enough. But UpperDog understands how partnership works. He understands that a prayer is neither a coax nor a command,

A prayer is a *variable*.

What happens in this life is always the culmination of many variables. The biggest variable in play, of course, is the active will of the Father. Praying in contradiction to his will, no matter how earnest, is not productive. That's why learning to listen is so imperative.

Another variable is our own will and the will of those for whom we are praying. My prayers for the salvation of a rebellious son, for instance, are mixed in with his own active rebellion. There is still free will at play. Variables are in constant competition and constant conglomeration.

Another variable is gifting, as we discussed in the section about calling. What happens as a result of a particular prayer is influenced by one's gifting. If I have gifting in power and miracles, my prayer to generate a limb or manifest resources or stop the rain carries a different kind of weight than if my gifting is in wisdom.

Faith is also a variable. Scripture is clear about that. As we've established so far, we don't want to err on the passive or the aggressive side of the faith variable. If faith is substantive but not sovereign (as we established in Chapter 8,) then how does it work? What are the mechanisms of collaborating with God?

The Faith Of Giants

I always wondered longingly about the difference between "regular" Christians like me and those rare giants of faith, who could pray and see things happen, lay on hands and see miracles. Discussions of faith made it sound like if I just believed more, I could bridge that gap. But how does one believe more? Belief always seemed one-dimensional to me. You either believe in God or you don't. Black or white, yes or no. How do you believe *more*? There was no apparent gradient involved.

And then God called me into my work. Splankna Therapy deals with the subatomic level of creation and how it relates to healing. Without realizing it, and mostly accidentally, I've spent over a decade and a half developing faith. It took quantum physics to open my eyes to some of faith's *mechanisms*. God showed me some of that ground between my experience of veritable impotence in prayer and the biblical assumption of power and effectiveness. Much of the trouble was that I had no idea what was happening when we pray. I really did pray like I was begging God to move, even though I knew better of his character. What I learned is that the "greater belief" that serves the effectiveness of prayer is not belief *in God*. Even in childhood I knew who God was. I knew his self-descriptions in the Word, his power, his love, his nearness. I believed he could do anything.

But I did not believe he *would*.

I did not honestly expect him to move. That kind of belief I had to develop like a skill. His Word says that he moves. It says he responds to prayer. These are propositions we would all adhere to. But moving proposition into reality is a process. The faith required for effective partnership is more like a skill that has to be developed, more skill than simple fact. The real challenge is to develop an honest expectation that our prayers carry weight. We've talked about listening because if I can hear him say something, I can have greater confidence that when I pray in line with that idea, it is productive—something happens. We discussed gifting and calling because again, the clearer I am on my gifting and the call on my life, the more I can actually believe, really expect that praying and moving in alignment with that calling is constitutive; it creates. We talk about authority because the understanding of Jesus' authority and ours in him increases our intentionality in prayer. We talk about our life experiences because experience feeds expectation.

These are the things that serve faith.

There was a moment when Jesus marveled. He was stunned. He had "never seen such faith in all of Israel!"[107] Do you remember it? A Gentile centurion, yes, not even a follower of Yahweh, asked Jesus to heal his servant. When Jesus was near his home, the centurion sent his servants out ahead. He sent them with a message. "Tell Jesus that he doesn't need to come under my roof. He only needs to say the word and I know my servant will be healed." When Jesus heard this he was stopped in his tracks. This man had such a clear understanding of authority and how it works, such a rich experience of seeing an authoritative word carried out, that he had developed faith. He knew how authority worked and he knew Jesus had it because he had already heard of his exploits. He honestly expected Jesus' word to accomplish the deed and Jesus called that "greater faith than all of Israel."

Part of the inner workings of Splankna Therapy (that we use in healing ministry), is the "moving" of things like destructive lies and vows in the soul out of where they've been lodged and placing them under the foot of the cross. Now I did not sit down seventeen years ago when Splankna's development began with the honest expectation that I could command things around in someone's soul and they would move. But I do now. Why? Because I believe in God more? No. Because little by little, like drops in a bucket over many years, my experience has shown me that when I pray that way, something happens. Without realizing it, I was developing faith.

Faith is not positional like authority. When we are "in Christ,"[108] we all have the same positional authority. We have all "been seated with Jesus at the right hand of the Father, high above all powers, rulers,"[109] whether baby Christian or aged. We all have the same position of authority, but not all of us can *enact* that authority to the same degree. To act in authority is a skill. It requires development. If you went to Disneyland this weekend and perused the vast sea of haggard, sun-stroked humanity, you would witness this reality. Every parent there has the same positional authority over their children, right? Fact is fact. And yet there is a very wide range of skill in *wielding* that authority. Some parents have their children in peaceful, ardent line. One sideways glance from Mom and they straighten up and fly right. But you'll see the other type as well—the exhausted, beaten parent who's getting walked all over by tiny, screaming banshees demanding world domination in the form of yet another stick of cotton candy. But each of these parents has the same positional authority.

Faith is the same way. It is a skill one grows into once the basic truths are established. Once the factual belief in God, in the truth of the Gospel is in place, the enacting of faith is developmental. I imagine that it didn't take all three years of hanging out with Jesus for the apostles to realize the *fact* of who he was. They knew fairly quickly that he was the Messiah (even though they had a different expectation of how that identity would manifest). I would guess that fairly early on they came to believe in *who* he was. They knew he was the Son of God. They knew he was a healer. But what does the ground look like between belief in who Jesus was, and the ability to say to the lame man at the gate, "Walk!" Peter actually expected the man to walk. He didn't hope he would. He didn't say, "Please, please, please Jesus." Or "Here, come with me and I'll take you to Jesus. He can heal you." No, he said, "What I have I give you." What I "*have?*" Seriously? Faith is the honest expectation that what I pray carries weight, that it is substantive *because* of who Jesus is and who he's made me to be. Peter believed that Jesus had given him that authority. He believed he had "walk" to give.

Because of the natural challenge of my work, I have developed an actual, honest expectation that when I sit down with a fellow believer and take authority over a lie or a traumatic memory for example, and pull it out of the soul and set it under the feet of Jesus, it actually moves in physical space. What I'm praying *occurs*. But I didn't wake up one morning with the ability to do that. Was my factual authority in Jesus in place twenty years ago? Of course, and so is yours. But I had to learn faith. I had to grow it like a muscle. I had to slowly build the honest expectation that my prayers were carrying weight—that it mattered what I thought or spoke.

One time in conversation with God I was marveling at those in history (and presently) who walk in power. I was feeling a little sorry for myself actually. I was telling him how I feel like a bit of a Christian stepchild at times because I don't experience the Spirit working through me in miracles. I feel so awed and small when I read stories of those who have regenerated limbs and felt ligaments move under their hands. As I whined, I felt like God chuckled at me. Have you ever felt like God's laughing at you? It's odd and funny. I felt him confront my pity party with, "Don't you know? *They* would be amazed at how *you* can command things around in a person's soul!" he said. Oh, I never thought of that. He was saying that while others may have developed faith for physical healing, they would not bring such a secure expectation to a prayer to move the heart. He continued, "The only reason you can't feel a ligament move under your hand is because you don't think you can." And he was right, of course. I don't come to prayer for physical healing with nearly the kind of honest expectation that I bring to prayers for the soul. My experience is built up in one camp, but not the other. I really do come to physical healing prayers with more doubt than expectation.

So, if this is true, if faith requires honest expectation, then we're back to that dilemma we discussed earlier. With most of our life experience of ineffective prayer stacked against us, how do we come to a new moment of prayer with an *honest* expectation that it carries weight; that something happens because of it? Even if we can get our minds and hearts fully around authority, gift and calling, hearing and moving, our experience is still powerful. If our life experience contradicts faith because we've seen a million "unanswered" prayers, that experiential load will still hold us back. How can we turn that tide? How can we pray like UpperDogs?

Well, because we work with the subatomic level of creation in our ministry, we have an unusual offering to this dilemma. We have peeked behind the quantum curtain and learned something wonderful. We've gotten a little gist of what *happens* when we pray, and it also serves the development of faith. When you understand a little bit about creation at its smallest level, possibilities open up and scriptural truths crystalize. So, in a curious conversational turn for a book on theology, let's look at quantum physics for a moment.

(Warned you.)

Schrödinger's Dog

Now it needs to be said, before we go any further, that we do not, by any means, have the line on faith. We are in process just like everyone else. Don't think for a second that we write all of this from a position of grand arrival. We share these ideas in hopes that they'll spark the same ambitions in you that they spark in us. Part of the reason we're so, well, sparky, is because of the specific take on the world that the Lord has called us to investigate: the subatomic level of creation. In the first book of this series, we presented a thumbnail explanation of quantum physics and in order to continue our UpperDog discussion of faith, we need to return to the topic here because it pertains to faith and the mechanisms of it's development. Believe it or not, understanding quantum physics also serves faith. So here goes... quantum physics 101.

You're familiar with the atom, right? You know that everything in creation is made up of atoms. Well it turns out that atoms have something to say about faith and its mechanisms, about what's *happening* when we pray.

Up until we split one of those atoms in order to create the atomic bomb in 1945, the global scientific community was under the impression that the atom was the smallest building block of creation.

Physics is the study of matter and its movement through space and time. Up until the atom was split, we had what is referred to as Newtonian, Galilean or macrophysics. This is the study of the big stuff, from the atoms and up. Physics is all based on mathematics, and the math works perfectly. The math at macro level, the level of the big stuff, teaches us about force and inertia. It enables us to build engines that move cars. It explains gravity and the rotation of planets.

The properties of macrophysics (the big stuff) seem fixed. For instance, physicists can show mathematically that if we can know two things about an atom—its position and velocity (speed)—then we can accurately predict its eventual outcome. Did you catch that? Everything in the universe is made of atoms, right? And physics can prove that if we know enough information about any particular atom, we can accurately predict its eventual outcome (meaning where it will eventually end up in space and time).

This is an incredible proposition. This implies that the whole universe, made up of all these little atoms, is *predictable*. This observation of creation gave support to such theological movements as Deism and Calvinism because it appeared that if there is a creator God, he just set his creation into motion and left it to its course— like everything is mathematically scripted and predetermined. The math of macrophysics makes it look like neither God, nor man plays a significant role in reality. (Sounding familiar yet?) The idea of extreme predestination, where man has nothing to contribute whatsoever in his salvation or damnation, appears true if all is predictable. Macrophysics would paint God as active in the story only it its inception and takes man out of the equation entirely.

But then we split those atoms open and the whole game changed.

At the subatomic or quantum level of creation (meaning everything smaller than the atoms), several astounding properties emerge, each remarkable in its own right. The first of these properties is emptiness. When we open up an atom we find that it is mostly empty. Isn't that surprising? Everything we experience as solid is made up of mostly empty space. What we find inside is a whole lot of space and an extremely small nucleus formed of protons and neutrons. Another fun property at this tiny level is the contradiction in the math itself. At the macro level, the physics math is perfect. Works every time. And at the subatomic level the math is just as pristine.

Both sets of math are works of art. But while they are both perfect, they are also perfectly inconsistent with each other! As far as our human theories have so far developed, we cannot conceive of any possible way that both sets of math can be true at the same time, and yet they are! How fun is that? You know when we split the atom that God must have been on the edge of his seat, "Just wait. You guys are going to love this!" Since this discovery, the world of physics has been in pursuit of what they call "unified field theory." They're all in a mad dash to see who will be the first to discover the equation that explains the apparent contradiction and makes it possible for both realities to co-exist.

Here's another one: there is a list of established qualifications in science for something to be classified as "matter" and conversely, a list of qualifications for something to be qualified as "information." The behavior of subatomic particles fits the "information" list better. This implies that the fundamental building blocks of everything are more like information, ideas, potentials, than fixed matter. Are we having fun yet? See one of the many wonderful books on Information Theory to explore that further.[110]

Indestructibility is another noteworthy quality of things at the subatomic level. Physics shows us that matter can neither be created nor destroyed, only moved around or transformed. Nothing ever truly disappears. It makes me think of how Scripture tells us that on that day we will give an account of every individual word we have spoken. They are things and they don't go away. It also makes me think about the blood of Jesus. Agnes Sanford muses that considering that matter cannot be destroyed, the literal blood of Jesus that was spilled on the cross is still in existence in our physical world. His blood fell to the ground, mixed with the dirt, changed form by turning to dust and dispersed into the universe. You and I probably breathe in and out the very particles of his own blood. Cool.

The next amazing property of the subatomic world begins to apply directly to our discussion. At the quantum level, everything is in motion. Our perception of steady state at the macro level, of something being not only solid but still, is a macro-illusion. If we could put on our quantum glasses and see it at its smallest level we would find it in frantic buzz. Now the physicists, coming upon this realization of quantum movement are struck with a problem. We already know from the macrophysics math that in order to have movement, you must have force. Remember your high school physics? "Inertia: an object in motion will tend to stay in motion. An object at rest will tend to stay at rest." Nothing can be in motion unless force is applied to it. And at the subatomic level, there is no explanation for what's causing the motion. There is no known force. How can everything be moving if nothing's pushing it?

If you didn't start with a Creator theology, you would have no intellectually cogent answer. Subsequently, physicists decided, "Well, whatever it is that's causing all the particles to move, we'll call it 'energy'." "Energy," the word that strikes fear and suspicion in so many believing hearts, is really just a physics term for whatever it is that's causing all the particles to buzz!

Now, as Christians, we know very well what's causing everything to be in motion—the active, ongoing will of God. Everything's moving because he wills it to. And the moment he no longer wills it to, it will stop. New age philosophy jumps to a false conclusion when they read about this mysterious, quantum movement. They teach, "This 'energy' IS god. It's what we've been saying all along!" they retort. "What everyone's always called "god" is really just this universal nebulous force that makes up the planets, thoughts, and you yourself. Therefore, you are god as well. You are the stuff of the divine and there is nothing more to him than that." New age thinking depersonalizes God into a force, and since that force is permeating all things, you are god, the tree is god, the rock is god, and so forth.

But the fact that the world makes a false conclusion doesn't require us to throw out the observation itself. Creation reveals what it reveals no matter what is concluded. As believers we know that while God does animate all things, while he does cause everything to buzz, that is far from the sum of him. He remains, his word explains clearly, distinct from his creation, higher than it and sovereign over it. The first book in this series, *Splankna*,[111] will take you into a deeper journey through these issues. Another wonderful resource is *The Physics of Heaven*[112] by Judy Franklin & Ellyn Davis. But for now, let's just enjoy this mysterious motion as a part of his work, a part of his ongoing will and explore what it means for us.

Another property at the subatomic level is that the "stuff" inside the atoms changes in state from wave to particle and back to wave again in a quite unpredictable way, much like the behavior of light. (One familiar with the Word can't help but be reminded of John 1:4, "in Him was life and that life was the light of the world," or "I am the light of the world," in John 8:12.) When subatomic substance is in the form of a wave, it is in what's called a "superposition." This means that it is in a state of pure potential. Only when it "collapses" into a particle does it become real, material.

"Schrödinger's Cat" is a famous quantum philosophy that illustrates this unpredictable state-change behavior of creation at the tiniest level. (I know we're going deep here but hang on. It really does apply to our discussion.) Basically Dr. Schrödinger explained in 1935 that if you put a cat in a sealed box that contained a vile of poison, you would have to concede that while the box remains sealed, the cat is potentially both alive and dead at the same time. He was giving a simple example of pure potential.

Now here's the point—one more astonishing property. At this level of creation, thought and emotion seem to have some kind of substance, like a frequency or signature resonance. Thoughts seem to have weight. Surprisingly, it is our *attention towards* a wave that causes it to "collapse" into a particle.

This is best illustrated by what's called the "Heisenberg Uncertainty Principle."[113] In short, this describes how at the quantum level we are not able to know both a particle's position and its velocity at the same time (like we need to know at the macro level in order to predict its eventual outcome). The *reason* we cannot know both at the same time is the really incredible thing. As far as physicists can tell, the reason we cannot know a particles position and velocity at the same time is because,

*our observation of the particles **affects** them.*

Our observation, our attention toward a particle, causes it to instantly "collapse." You see, before we observe the particle, it isn't a particle at all. It's a wave. It is in its "wave state," meaning that it is pure potential. It can collapse into a fixed particle anywhere in space or time. Only when we observe it does it "pop" into a fixed particle. Because our observation changes its state from wave to particle, we are unable to objectively examine it.

Now that should make your head spin. You should probably read it again. When we focus our attention on the stuff that makes up everything—observe it, shine a light on it, measure it, think our thoughts at it—it is changed. So changed that our intention towards it destroys objectivity. It's like trying to see your own profile in a single-paned mirror. You can turn your head to the side, and you know that at that moment your profile is reflected in the mirror accurately. But the second you try to look at that reflection, it is no longer your profile. Your attention has changed the image fundamentally. Unless you have several mirrors at once, you cannot look at your own profile. The observation itself changes the image.

In his wonderful book, *Quantum Glory*,[114] Phil Mason explains in great detail these astounding subatomic properties and how they align with biblical teaching. One proposal he makes is particularly noteworthy. He explains this property of observation affecting the particles; how everything exists as waves, in pure potential form until observed, and then they "pop" into a solid particle. He then raises this question: "so if nothing can exist in solid form unless it is observed, how does the universe stay in place when no one's looking?" How can a chair remain a chair when no one is observing it and causing its waves to become particles? He proposes that the answer to this dilemma is the observation of God himself. It is God who is always observing everything. God is the ultimate observer holding all things together. Within his ultimate organizing observation is allowed our space to also co-effect the waves and particles. Our impact is only known within the super-structure of his own. (Okay, by now you've *got* to be having fun.)

Remember how the biblical worldview is racked with paradox? One of those is the apparent paradox of predestination vs. free will. In our limited human understanding, it seems impossible for both of these to be true at once. To our understanding, we would either have to be predestined OR free to choose, but we couldn't be both. The subatomic superposition reality relates to this conundrum. The tiny side of creation implies that all things are existing in lively, open potential; that our freedom is real. It is only God's unique existence outside of time that allows him to both allow our authentic freedom and still know its outcome. (But that's another book.)

So let's get back to our discussion of faith. Each of these properties of creation is pregnant with theological implication, but let's look more closely at the last two especially:

If everything is made up of little buzzing particles,
And it is the active will of God that keeps them buzzing,
And my attention also affects them,
Then by God's design,

I am an active player in this story.

I affect things. I contribute constantly. The wild paradigm shift that quantum discovery affords believers is that we are meaningful players, unavoidably. Regardless of your theological bend, the creation itself testifies to your significance. The truth is that every thought you've ever had, every emotion you've ever felt, every expectation, hope or fear

has been impacting the particles around you,

the particles that make up everything. You are a point of influence. God has designed a human being as a contributor... a significant, constant, measurable mover in the story. Whether we know him or not, we are constantly impacting reality. We are constantly feeding into the story. In every moment we are utilizing those built-in potentials in God's grand stage. We don't create out of nothing like he does, but we are constantly influencing.

I used to be deeply bothered by prayer studies. Have you read them? In the medical community they have a habit of setting up studies on prayer where they gather people of all different faiths, or no faith at all, and assign them to patients in the hospital. They give them the assignment to pray for healing for some period of time. There is also a group receiving no prayer at all. They're looking to see if prayer does anything. The vast majority of these studies conclude that prayer does indeed make a difference in the prognosis of illness. Those who receive prayer heal faster. But this finding has always puzzled me. How could the prayers of an unbeliever be effective? Looking back now, I can see where I got stuck. My old underdog theology was that prayer was a means of coaxing God, remember? So how could an unbeliever coax a God he doesn't know? Now I understand those studies so much better. All men are contributors by design, whether they know their Creator or not. All intention lands. Well-wishes carry weight. They are a variable, even if small.

This is both a profound privilege and a profound responsibility. Yes, the enemy distorts this reality in the secular mind, just like he does with all other truth. Rather than simply standing in awe at our position as partners with God, the world says, "No, quantum physics proves that you are THE mover. YOU are sovereign. Since you're impacting the particles, that means that *everything* that happens in your life you manifested. You're not a partner with a sovereign God. You are the one in charge." And we're right back to the garden with the original temptation, "You can be like God." (See the Splankna book for a thorough discussion of the new age response to quantum physics vs. the biblical one.)[115]

The new age distortion is powerful and sneaky and critical to avoid. But lie aside; we really need to consider further the implications of this partnership. In the first book we looked at it in terms of the profound responsibility—the incredible eye-opener it is to know that my every thought is carrying weight. But here, let's go on to look at the profound privilege. How does this quantum reality relate to faith? What does it mean to be contributors?

Drops In A Bucket

Under the big umbrella of the professional, psychological world, there is a burgeoning sub-field called "energy psychology." It comes at the idea of emotional healing from a different angle. It works off of the observation that at the subatomic level, thoughts and emotions have some kind of weight or frequency. Rather than talking a person through an issue, or giving them an experience to help them resolve their emotional trauma and their psychological maladaptive symptoms, energy psychology comes in through the body door. Theoretically, the body stores all of one's life experiences like a hard drive. Every emotion, thought, memory, belief etc. is stored like an electrical charge in the body. We are all walking conglomerations of everything we've ever known. Energy psychology assists the body in letting go of the trauma roots that are fueling symptoms, by ascertaining and resolving them like electrical charges. (See Chapter 15 here, or *Splankna* [116] for more explanation.)

The fact that the body and heart are capable of healing in this way is just another example of God's unsearchably beautiful creation. The problem with the field of energy psychology is that its practitioners have only developed their tools from a secular, Eastern and new age worldview. The call on the Splankna Institute has been to develop and utilize this level of creation and its healing potential from a passionately biblical worldview. The ins and outs of accomplishing that were covered in detail in the first book.[117] In our Level 1 trainings we teach fellow believers how to work with this aspect of God's creation to relieve physically stored trauma in those they work with. The focus there is on healing. But now it's time to discuss how the subatomic level of creation informs faith and its development. What do subatomic particles whisper about the fabric of things, the creative side of things? Let's look at the creative potential of this remarkable paradigm: thoughts and emotions have substance.

What do the discoveries in Quantum Physics whisper to us about partnership with God?

What Is Happening When We Pray

So much of why the church has lost hope in prayer is because we have not understood the mechanisms underlying it. We have not understood what is happening when we pray. We have childishly looked at prayer like a light switch. I ask God for "x." If "x" doesn't happen, then either it wasn't his will for it to happen, or somehow I'm a failure for not asking harder. What we haven't understood is that the weaving interplay of partnership means that every time we think, every time we pray, we are contributing. The partnering process is continuous. And the variables are always in play.

Think of it like paint in a bucket. Let's say my husband's life was a bucket full of white paint originally, but then his anger at God and rebellion has slowly been dropping little black drops into his bucket, one by one, over many years. By now it's a fairly dark shade of gray. When I embark on the campaign to pray for his salvation, my first prayer is like a new drop of bright yellow into that deep gray mix.

If I drop my yellow, it does have an impact. It can't help it. The hue changes. But maybe only slightly. Each drop I offer continues to change that hue. Depending on several variables, like the ones we've discussed—my own maturity in Christ, my level of developed faith, my spiritual gifting and calling, my embracing of authority, my life experience, etc.—my drops may be bigger or smaller,

but they're never *nothing.*

Those tiny particles show us that. My drops in his bucket, my love and longing and request for my husband before the Lord *cannot* go void. Quantum physics proves it! Thoughts are things! Every one of them lands by creation's design. Obviously God remains sovereign. Nothing I contribute can skate past his allowance. But he is the one who designed us as contributors. How *heavily* my contributions lands is a variable that co-mingles with many others. Years ago I could've prayed the same words in prayer that I pray today with clients and they would've landed, but not as heavily as they do now. That is because of the variable of honest expectation that I now bring to the table, the variable of faith that has been built like a multi-varied muscle over time.

Let's say, on the other hand, that my mother-in-law is devoted to Jesus and has been pouring color into a particular issue for quite some time. It may be my one single drop in agreement with hers that tips the balance far enough for it to manifest in measurable result. It's finally more pink than brown. Maybe in another circumstance that white bucket only got a tiny amount of dark green dropped in and a small color addition is enough to repair it. If we understood that our prayers are contributions in our partnership with God, we would be much more invested in prayer. Every one of them lands. Every prayer contributes and makes a difference in the fabric of reality. It's just that not every contribution is the one that causes the visible effect on the surface. Prayers are both substantive and cumulative. Revelation 5:8 describes the twenty-four elders before the throne of God. They are "holding golden bowls full of incense, which are the prayers of the saints."

Donation Matching

Not only are our prayers substantive and cumulative, but when we are praying within his will, we experience something like donation matching. You've heard it on the radio during pledge week, right? "For every dollar you pledge to our station, the so-and-so organization will contribute 10." This mutuality exists between God and mankind and within the Trinity itself. Scripture mentions that there were moments when Jesus "knew that the Spirit was present for healing,"[118] implying that there were times when the Spirit was not present for healing. Jesus knew when the Spirit was ready to join him in power for healing, to match his donation. Again, the dynamic, specific will of the Father, who generally wills healing, was a living variable in the moments of Jesus' life.

And then with us the mutuality continues. Remember what happened when Jesus went back to his hometown of Nazareth? Astoundingly, the Scriptures tell us that he was "unable" to do any miracles there because of their lack of faith! Jesus? Unable? That's what it says.

That statement implies a few interesting things. First of all, Jesus apparently wanted to do miracles there, or the Scripture would have said that he chose not to, or simply that he didn't. Instead, it says that he was unable. How often does God prefer to work a miracle and finds in us elements that render him unable? Secondly, it implies that it was their lack of faith that caused him to be unable. It does not say that he chose not to do miracles as a punishment for their heart posture, but that the posture itself was the hindrance.

The Scripture testifies that our measure of faith is a substantive variable in what happens. We offer, and he offers even more and together forms the story. No one in Nazareth was willing to engage him in the donation-matching dance. They had nothing to offer him, nothing he could respond to and multiply. In fact, the implication is that their offering was negative. Their indignance at his messianic claim not only failed to invite him, but actively blocked him.

When we play with this analogy of donation matching an interesting question arises. What about the unbeliever? Since we've already established that every thought and emotion pours into reality, contributes, then what happens with an unbeliever's contributions? An unbeliever is constantly contributing to reality too. The difference is at worst rebellion and at best isolation from partnership with God. The unbeliever is contributing because he cannot help it. He is designed that way by God. He is a point of influence naturally whether or not he knows his creator. The difference is that he is contributing in a vacuum. The unbeliever does not know how to pour into the desires of the Lord. He does not usually experience the great donation matching of the Father unless he happens to accidentally line up with his will (such as in the prayer studies). But UpperDog knows that when he prays in alignment with the will of the Father, "he has what he asks." The father responds, whether this particular donation was the breakthrough-manifesting drop or not.

God himself speaks of this donation-matching interaction literally when he calls his people to trust him with the tithe. They are worried. They do not feel like they can afford to bring in the tithe, but he says, "Test me in this! See if I will not throw open the floodgates of heaven!"[119] "If you will bring your offering, I will match it like crazy!"

Mark was diagnosed with terminal cancer and with only weeks to live. He had been declining slowly for a few years, but now it was close to the end and everyone knew it. On one particular Sunday morning, the preacher suggested that we gather around and pray for him. The different flavors of Christian tradition have their own strengths and weaknesses. My own Christian heritage was strong in knowledge of the Word and in loving one another. But the main weakness was in cessationism—the belief that the work of the Holy Spirit in power ended with the apostles. So gathering together to lay on hands and pray for healing was not customary for this particular group of Christians. But we all loved Mark very much and it would be so wonderful… right?

So everyone stood up and shuffled awkwardly around Mark's chair. We formed one of those human prayer webs around him and someone prayed on behalf of the group. There were probably about two hundred of us and there was a great deal of love in that moment. But there was not as much faith. If faith is the honest expectation that something will *happen* because of a prayer, then we were on the slim side. Again, it's not something anyone would say out loud, but while we would love to see God heal Mark, no one really expected him to stand up whole. We pray more like a social courtesy, a gesture of compassion. We pray half-hearted, feeble things like, "be with the doctors." You've been there.

I was standing near the outside of the group, and as the prayer came to an end and everyone began to meander back to their seats, I unexpectedly heard God speak. He said,

"You bought him a year."

I froze. Did I really hear that? It was very difficult for me to accept that I had heard that from God. I come from the passive side of things, remember? I stood there trying to process. It seemed that God was saying that our combined mustard seeds of faith, as small as they were, were received by the Lord, matched and landed. Our prayers made a difference—a year's difference.

Mark died one year later.

I was so disrupted by this experience that I didn't share it with anyone. Not even my husband. Truthfully, it was even difficult for me to share it with Heather for the writing of this book. It seems so offensive. I especially stumble over the word "bought." But I can't skirt the issue. That's what he said. I had to deal with it.

The variable of our offering for Mark mixed in with other variables: Mark's own will, the momentum of the cancer itself, and probably other variables as well. But apparently our prayers made a dent, a dent that was literal and measurable. When we were praying, the situation was not God answering our request with a simple "yes" or "no." There were variables involved and we were joining in. The very composition of subatomic creation attests to these variables… the constant mixing of potentials.

Now, I realize what a threatening proposition this is. If you have tended toward the passive side you're offended right now and if you're on the aggressive side you're saying, "See!" But hang in here with me. I'm actually suggesting that the middle ground is true, the dynamic tension we've discussed. What if our prayers are literal, cumulative contributions to the will of God? Not in charge, but constitutive? If our prayers bought Mark a year, then theoretically, if we had continued to contribute, he may have been healed if that was God's desire.

Don't hear me saying that this is true in every case. That's aggressive. I'm not saying that every time someone ends up dying it was because we didn't contribute enough prayer. "It is appointed that every man should die." There is such a thing as God answering, "No." What I am suggesting is that God does not control everything like a chess game. If he did, if he controlled everything to follow his perfect desires, then why would he ask us to pray? Why wouldn't he just say, "You guys just sit and watch. I'll do what I want."

I'm suggesting that there are times when he has a desire that does not come about because his children did not join him in it. "If my people would only pray, *then* I would…"[120] He has arranged things so that our contribution is not only useful, it is necessary. This is exactly why we fall into passivity or aggression, because it is so difficult to accept the vulnerability of true partnership. God asks us to contribute, even though we cannot control the outcomes. We would rather it be that we're either in control, or out of the game. But that is not intimate. And intimacy is his top priority. He is not fundamentally power. He is love.

What if partnership means contributing our prayers, our honest expectation, our cries before him and tolerating all the while that the final decision will remain in his hands? Not ducking out and not demanding. Offering.

Offering my heart out because I know my contributions count. They accumulate and affect the particles. Things will happen because of them that would not have happened otherwise.

And he will still be God.

(Keep in mind our discussion in Chapter 8 about declaration paranoia. Keep the balance here. Remember that while our thoughts are things and they do it like a variable added into a big mixing

pot over which God is ultimately sovereign. Don't fall off the other side of this wagon into hyperventilating if you speak a negative word. Just don't be characterized by it. Be characterized by the expectation of life and gratefulness.)

That said, this glimpse into quantum reality assists us in faith. How? Because if I'm stuck in that dilemma or poor experience with prayer, and I don't come to a new moment of prayer with the honest expectation that something will happen (i.e. in the posture of unproductive doubt), I do still have three productive options. What we've discussed here is the first one:

1. I can be confident that my offering did _something_.

Even if only incremental, because I know that thoughts are things. They are unable to be void. All intention lands. My prayer *had* to do something. It has no choice. The confidence that my prayer did something, the confidence that understanding the subatomic nature of thoughts affords me, assists faith. It gives me a legitimate reason to trust, to know beyond a shadow of a doubt that my prayer mattered. It was a thing. It was a drop in that bucket no matter how small. That confidence gives faith some substance to grow on. Before knowing about the quantum level of things, my ideas, my words just seemed like vapors. If nothing popped into visual existence in that moment, it all seemed for naught. But UpperDog knows better.

Imagination and Prayer

Now let's look at the second option at our disposal when faith needs assistance:

2. I can imagine.

Someone interviewed Agnes Sanford, a well-known Christian author, shortly after the end of World War II. The little village where she lived had sent many boys off to war but each one, to the number, had returned home safely. This statistic aroused a flurry of news curiosity. The interviewer asked Agnes what sense she made of the phenomenon. She replied simply, "Well, we know how to pray." Wow. Don't you want to kidnap her and strap her to a chair in your dining room until she tells you what she knows? I do.

She wrote an unassuming little paperback in 1945 called *The Healing Light*[121] that changed the way I pray. She was a woman who walked in a profound gift of physical healing in the Holy Spirit. It was commonplace for her to see the truly miraculous kind of healing. She describes laying her hand on someone's broken knee and feeling the bones and ligaments moving under her fingers while she prayed. The book shared many of these accounts, and some of what she had learned over the years about the mechanisms of healing, prayer and faith. She shares with the reader several patterns she observed. Most significantly, she noticed that if she imagined the thing she was praying for as she prayed it, it seemed to be useful.

Simple enough idea, right? Imagine what you're praying and it's useful. But have you ever heard a sermon on imagination? When I read that, I was stunned by the realization that in my entire life, growing up in a denomination that placed heavy emphasis on knowing Scripture, and even throughout earning my degree in Bible, I had never once heard a teaching on the role of imagination in the life of a believer. How can that be? We are the only part of God's entire creation that even *has* imagination. Surely that's not an accident. Surely he put it there for a significant purpose. The only discussion I had ever heard or read about imagination was from the cautionary side. Discussion of how our imagination is dangerous, used for evil, runs a-muck and how we must keep it in check. I had never once heard about its godly purpose. God's expansive intentions are wider than I can ever grasp. What he means imagination to be used for is probably so much wider than I've ever considered, but this much I know:

Imagination is bandwidth.

When we offer our imagination to God, he *uses* it. Our imagination is part of the mechanism of partnership with God. Imagination is creative. We've already established that our thoughts have weight, that they feed into the quantum field and effect reality around us. God has designed us this way. It's part of our mechanisms of participation. Our imagination is especially weighty. When we imagine, the impact is measurable. Studies in neurobiology have shown that when a subject sees an object, let's say a baseball, certain firings go off in the neuro-network. If they then take away the baseball and ask the subject to imagine a baseball, the very same firings go off in the brain. Your brain doesn't know the difference between seeing a baseball and imagining one! Imagination carries heavy frequencies.

Another important feature of imagination is that it is free. What do I mean by that? Imagination is not bound like our emotions are. I can imagine anything any time. My emotions, on the other hand, are not free. I feel what I feel. I can't make myself feel something that isn't true. I cannot force emotions to line up like I want them to. If I'm terrified of my upcoming trip to the dentist, I can't decide to feel confident about it and "voila!" Human emotions are not so easily contrived. I can act like a confident person and that will help draw my emotions along, but I can't simply decide to feel something and make it happen. But no matter what, my imagination remains free. It is unbounded. While I may not be able to make myself feel something in particular,

I am always able to imagine it.

I can imagine anything, no matter how I feel. I can't make myself feel strong self-worth for instance if my life experience has beaten that out of me. But I can *imagine* being someone with strong self-worth. I can imagine, "What if I did feel worthy? What would I think like, respond like?" The imagination is unfettered. I am always free to imagine anything within the scope of human experience, even beyond that into wild arenas of invention and potential. This incredible capacity is an integral part of our being "made in his image."[122] We are the only part of creation given this honor, and part of its uniqueness is the quality of imaginative capacity.

Understanding the quantum description of thoughts having weight puts meat on the possible reason for our unique, imaginative ability. What if imagination was given to us to serve reigning? The probable fact is that every time you imagine anything, whether of life or death, you are not only retraining your neuro-network, but you are also pouring into reality, adding a line in the story. Our imagination is meant to be used purposefully as a means of contribution. Everything I imagine is reflected in the physiological training of my body, and in the affecting of the particles around me. Imagination feeds gifting, making plans, finding possibilities, productivity in every arena. I am an unavoidable player in every second.

Let's return to our earlier established dilemma in faith. If faith is the honest expectation that what I pray makes something happen, based on who God is and who he's made me to be, then most of us don't pray in much faith. Our life experiences can work against us and suggest that nothing much happens when we pray, so we approach prayer with a confessed expectation of impact, but not an honest one. Because we pray in doubt as the Scriptures would describe it, or with no honest expectation of efficacy, our prayers may, in fact, land close to empty much of the time. That experience only reinforces the problem and the next opportunity to approach prayer begins with even less faith. I pray in doubt because my prayers don't accomplish much. And my prayers don't accomplish much because I pray in doubt! Therein lies the vicious cycle. I contend that the awareness of the constitutive impact of imagination, the weight of thoughts, offers us a way to throw a wrench in this repetitive pattern.

If my friend tears his ACL skiing and he asks me to pray for the Lord to heal it, and I'm the common Christian whose dilemma we're describing, I can lay my little hands on that knee and dive into the proper prayer language. I can close my eyes, furrow my brow and sound very faithful in my petition. But if I don't honestly expect something to happen, if my heart posture is planted squarely in doubt, Scripture has already foretold the outcome. "A man who prays and doubts should not expect to receive anything."[123] So I'm stuck. I can't force myself to honestly believe something will happen. But I do have another option at my disposal. I can *imagine* something happening. I can offer my imagination to God like bandwidth, understanding that every thought, no matter how small, carries weight. I can offer imagination even when I can't honestly expect change. Imagination is free and constitutive. It can create/contribute when faith is as yet under-developed. I may not be able to honestly believe that knee will move under my fingers (yet), but I can imagine it happening and honestly believe that my offering was *something*, that it can't help but be something because of my design, because of the fabric of creation. No thought, no emotion disappears. Thoughts are things. Each one lands. Doubt lands, faith lands, and so does imagination.

Imagination is like training wheels for faith.

We're discussing employing imagination in our prayers because imagination pours a heavy dose of color into that bucket. It's meant to. As a creature, made in his image, I'm designed to offer him my creative imaginative capacity as bandwidth to bring about his purposes in the world. It's one of the ways we're meant to contribute, to disseminate the Kingdom come. No matter what your level of faith may currently be,

SEE *what you pray.*

Every time. See what you pray as a means of offering God your partnership. The more you can see what you pray, the more creative, the more constitutive it lands. This is part of being his hands and feet. See what you pray and it carries more weight, drops a bigger drop. Any way you can think of to pray more visually, use it. It matters. If I'm going to give something to Jesus, like an old childhood wound for instance, and I'm going to entrust it to him and ask him to deal with it in healing, I won't say something like, "Jesus, I give you this issue. Please heal it." Now obviously that's a wonderful prayer, a wonderful thing to do. But I'll do it as visually as possible. I'd say something more like, "I wrap my hands around that old memory and I pull it up from anywhere it's been buried. I set it down into your hands Jesus and release it. Will you please crack it open now and expose it? Will you let the light of your face shine all over it? Will you take hold of it and work it soft, like the potter and the clay, until it's melted in your hands?" Just reading that, you saw so many images, didn't you? Of course you did. Anyone would. It's the natural way our minds work and we're made that way for a reason.

All that "seeing" just landed heavier on the particles than mere proposition would have. Imagination is one way to break ourselves out of that vicious cycle of prayer without faith. While I can't contrive honest expectation when I don't have it, faith when it isn't there, I can still imagine. I can imagine as an offering no matter how I feel. And when I do, I *can* honestly believe that my offering was *something.* That is caused incremental development, even if it was small, toward the will of God in that issue. If I were to do this on a regular basis, I would eventually begin to see the fruit of my contributions on the sensory level and then bolder faith begins to develop. Then the vicious cycle can eventually turn toward life. Then I can eventually come to a new moment of prayer and actually have the honest expectation for the miraculous; faith.

That's what Peter had at the gate.[124] He honestly expected the lame man to stand up and walk not because he was in a class by himself in faith that you and I can never reach, but because he had spent three full years watching miracle after miracle and it changed his honest expectations. *His* life experience taught him that yes, prayer *does* change things. And our employing of imagination in prayer is one way to move in that direction.

We can finally let go of the futile, false theology that says if one prayer didn't get it done, it must not have been the will of God. We can stop believing we're failures when nothing measurable happens. We can know that all our offerings were effective, even if not all offerings showed up on the macro lens.

It's a Set-Up

Underdog Christian sees the story of life as somewhat stacked against him. There are several ways that we seem set up to fail. I went through a season in my life when I really struggled with how the typical life story seems to be arranged. We're all born to fallen parents. We spend the first chunk of life getting wounded by them in whatever their special style might be. Then we spend the rest of our days in the painstakingly difficult attempt to heal from all that, only to die and have all things made new in the end anyway. Seems like we're all hamsters on a wheel. We're asked to trust in a God we can't see or hear, believe in a future we can't prove exists, and love a world full of people who betray and disappoint us regularly. Underdog can easily feel like he's set up to fail.

But subatomic creation disagrees.

Remember how we said that thoughts affect the particles? That emotions have substance? Something like weight? Well it turns out, they may not all weigh the *same*. The math seems to indicate that positive emotions literally weigh more than negative ones. We've established that thoughts impact reality. So when we think, feel or imagine, we create. Let's look at the body for an example. Every emotional state has a corresponding physiological profile. Every emotion creates a specific chemical balance in the brain, impact on heart rate and nervous system, hormonal signature, etc. At every given moment, my body is manifesting my emotional state in a myriad of ways. When I practice a habitual emotional state, let's say anxiety, my body literally learns those corresponding balances. They become like an easy default. Every cell in the body has receptors for each individual emotional neuropeptide. The more I "practice" a particular emotional state, the more my cells literally create new receptors for that emotion and kill off the ones that aren't getting used.

Caroline Leaf gives a thorough explanation of this psychophysiological machinery in her book, *Who Switched Off My Brain?*[125] The body is constantly being shaped by the soul. They mirror each other tightly. In the clinical research on depression, for instance, they can line up a hundred people who report depression and notice that they all have a similar chemical imbalance in the brain. They reason,

"It must be this chemical imbalance that causes depression. Let's give them the right medicine to correct the imbalance." But there is another reasonable deduction to make—that depression causes that particular chemical imbalance. You see, while the soul and body are in tight mutual mirroring, it is the soul that is predominant. The soul is directing the body for the most part, not the body directing the soul. Research shows that your neuropeptides (the emotion chemicals in your body) are being constantly redesigned. The ones you use multiply and the ones you neglect die off. Every cell in your body lives out its lifespan and is replaced.[126] *How* it is replaced, what shape a new cell will be in is affected by what think and feel. You're constantly contributing not only externally but internally as well.

Now Underdog would assume that if he spent twenty years "practicing" anxiety and building up all those physiological learned responses, it would take him at least another twenty years of "practicing" security or peace in order to override the anxiety wiring.

But here's the surprise...

It seems that positive emotions may be subatomically *heavier* than negative ones. They seem to hit with more impact on the particles, almost like positive emotions have a stronger frequency than negative ones. For instance, it only takes a little bit of practicing peace to trump years of practicing anxiety. A small investment in joy overrides a decade of bitterness. Isn't that great? We're set-up for life. Things are subatomically stacked in our favor.

Growing up in the Word, I became familiar with what a strong emphasis is placed on one's thought life. "If there is anything praise worthy, or beautiful....think on these things."[127] "Take every thought captive and make it obedient to Christ Jesus."[128] God knew all along that every thought was landing. He knew that every emotion was carrying weight and enacting our thorough partnership in the story. With all these Scriptures he was saying more than "be a good girl." He was saying, "With every thought you think, every emotion you feel, you are impacting reality. *Do it well!*"

I love John Piper's book, *Desiring God*.[129] He makes the provocative suggestion that the many, many times throughout the Bible where we are encouraged to "praise," "worship," and "exalt," God etc. can be accurately translated as meaning, "Enjoy Me!" Wouldn't that be a remarkable shift from how you've always read those injunctions? God can seem like something of an egomaniac with all those demands for accolade. But when you consider that he might be inviting us to *enjoy* him, the story changes. What if all those directions to praise him are really invitations to pleasure? Invitations to roll around in sloppy abandon to the unbelievable wonderfulness of our God, dreamily smiling all the while. God knows that our positive emotions are constitutive. He made them to be. He knows that when we engage pleasure and joy, especially in him, good things are being built. The particles are glowing.

Recently, when we were discussing this idea in one of our trainings, someone in the group asked, "If positive emotions are so much more powerful than negative ones, why aren't we all courageous and joyful?" Great question. The reason we're not all courageous and joyful is because while the deck is stacked in our favor, we're not utilizing it. We *don't* practice joy and courage. We practice, on that private, silent, internal plane, a whole host of negativity. Underdog has been forfeiting his advantage. But not anymore. Now you know, and you can never "un-know" it again. (Is that a word?)

There's More To Your Part

Remember how God told me there was more to my part than begging him? I described earlier in the book how that moment was such a revelation for me. I had truly never realized that my theology was built that way. I really did think that my part was to beg him. I beg, and if nothing happens, then I need to beg harder. But that night he said there was more to my part. It was one of the clearest words I've ever heard from him. So what is it? What's the rest of my part?

The rest of my part is to join him in bringing it about. Not just in my behavior (like exercising if I'm praying to lose weight), but in prayer as well. Once I've brought my request, my need before the Lord, I need to take the next step. I need to join him creatively in the answer. Deep grief, frustration and loss of hope have grown in the church because we have misunderstood this reality. So many of us have really lived like our only part in bringing things about is to beg him. But here's the secret. A begging posture is not productive. It is intimate, but not creative. There is nothing wrong with bringing my longing before the Lord. We are called constantly to do that. But we are not to stop there.

That night God did not say, "You're wrong for begging me." He did not say, "Your begging is blocking me." He said, "There's more." There's a next step. I needed to trust that he heard my plea, and then move into partnership on it. I needed to move beyond the request into productivity. So many of David's psalms exemplify this. He begins by throwing a fit before the Lord, sometimes in anger, sometimes in fear or desperation. But almost all of those psalms come full circle. David moves past that initial place and into gratefulness, worship and hope. He eventually moves into marveling at the greatness of the Lord, his good plans and his unfailing love.

He didn't stop at begging.

Now if you know the Word, you're reminded of the persistent widow, right? Jesus uses her as an example of how things work between God and us. He describes how the widow continually brought her request before an unjust, uncaring judge. Finally, out of sheer annoyance, the judge grants her request. Jesus is saying that surely if an ungodly judge will eventually relent to begging, your Father will treat you even better. He is not saying, "Beg harder, people!" He's saying trust the heart of your Father.

He is not reluctant.

When we remain, day after day, year after year in a begging posture towards the Father, we are saying we believe him to be reluctant or disinterested—an accusation he flatly denies. What if the reason our years of begging are unproductive is because we were meant to move past that stage with him? What if he's saying all along, "Yes, I hear you, let's do it." But we just keep bringing, "Please God, Please?"

Those little buzzing particles speak to this issue as well. It seems that negative emotions are energetically closed. Bitterness resists love. Desperation blocks abundance. When I feel desperate I should bring it to the Lord, of course. But not as leverage. My desperation is not my power to influence him. He is influenced by love, motivated by joy. I do not use my desperation as pressure on him. I admit it, bring it to him, repent of it (since I know the truth that he has the story handled), and then participate with him in its answer. How? Internally and externally.

Our external participation includes all of our acts of obedience and expectation. It's all of those behaviors that fit into the old adage, "If you pray for rain, bring an umbrella." On the aggressive side, there has been much discussion about this kind of external participation. There is no doubt that we have several scriptural examples (enough to constitute a pattern) of Jesus asking people to participate behaviorally in their moment of healing. "Stretch out your hand" he says to the man whose hand is crippled. It is in the act of stretching it out that the healing manifests. As long as these behaviors are done as contributions, as offerings to the Lord and not as demands, they are productive. When these acts come from a posture of manipulation, they become examples of aggressive theology. We have to remember that the individuals in Scripture received personal, literal directions from Jesus. If you hear Jesus tell you to stretch out your hand in faith, whatever that specific act might look like in your circumstance, do it! But if I have prayed to walk on water, I had better hear him say, "come," before I jump out of the boat. If I jump out because my act of "faith" will force his hand, I'm out of line. This is a subtle, personal heart posture issue. It may sound semantic, but it matters.

Our internal participation is what we really want to explore here. If God is who he says he is, if his character is trustworthy, if he is not hard of hearing, then he has received my request. After all, he "knows what I need before I ask it!" So there is no need for me to repeat it endlessly. There is no need to camp out in my desperation. The only desperation, the only longing to be embraced for its own sake is the longing for the God himself. Longing is like fear. It only has one rightful place—the Lord himself. The only time fear is ever endorsed in Scripture is when it's directed at God; awe and trembling before him. Longing is the same way. The only place our desperation is legitimate is when we are desperate for him.

Desperation for anything else creates a closing, blocking posture. Emptiness closes things in my heart and around me. Everything lands, remember? Faith and trust in the character of God frees me from the need to endlessly replay my emptiness before him. I can present my request and then offer my participation. I can imagine.

Let's say I'm praying for my teenage son who's struggling with suicidal thoughts. Naturally I'm afraid, right? I'm terrified by the thought of him killing himself and the overwhelming tragedy that would be. It is honest and intimate for me to bring that to the Lord. But what if that was all I brought? What if I continued day after day to bring deep worry and dread before the Lord and that was it? It would still be intimate but it would not be as productive. My worry does not produce life, not in my son and not in me. It does not produce fruit. It just reinforces itself. Worry begets worry and hope begets hope. It would be more productive to bring my worry before the Lord and lay it down like a sacrifice. Ask him to remove it and fill me with his own hope and plans for my son. And then I would go there with him.

I would employ my God-appointed imagination and put it to use. Remember: imagine as an offering, not a demand. That's what keeps you out of the aggressive imbalance. As a partnering offering, I would imagine the Love of the Father surrounding my son. I would see his arms around him and his love flowing into his broken heart. I would imagine hope sparking in my son and growing until it fills him. I would imagine conviction and insight waking up in my son's heart and mind, awakening him to the truth about this hole he's been digging. I would see his future full of strength and adventure. I would see the Lord accomplishing marvelous things out of this trial in my son's life. And the particles start glowing. God matches my donation like crazy and things move. Maybe slowly, maybe quickly. Remember, there are many variables in play. But God's own creation has shown me that my thoughts are things, that they land. I'm not going to continually pour the death-blow of dread over my son. That is not helpful. I'm going to participate in life. Remember when God showed Heather how to pray more productively for her brother Nick?

There is more to your part than begging him.

A Vision Not Realized

Many grieving, confused believers have experienced this. God seems to give a vision, a word, or an impression. Maybe it's a vision of a loved one being physically healed or a marriage restored or a child turning from rebellion and coming to faith. God gives the vision of the blessed thing to come. You *know* he did. You *know* it was from him. But somehow, inexplicably, it did not come to pass. The loved one died, the estranged spouse married someone else, the house foreclosed. What are we to make of this? Obviously, we doubt the original vision. Was that really God? Was it just my own heart's longing? It is a reasonable question. The answer to this disparity may very well be that your own heart conjured the hope in the first place. We know it cannot be that the Lord lied or failed.

But what if there is another option? What if the apparent inconsistency is because the original vision was taken as a "promise" when it was really an invitation—an invitation to join him in bringing the thing about? We receive these visions as promises, as guarantees, like God is saying, "Here's what's going to happen, no matter what you do." We rejoice over the vision and count on it. I think our hearts are noble in that. If the vision was a promise, that would be the proper response. But we have not even considered that what was shown to us *could* be something *other* than a promise. Could it be an invitation? Could the Lord be saying, "Here's what *can* be. Here's what I long for. Join me in creating it."

If you, the reader, have personally experienced a vision from the Lord that did not come to pass, please hear us say this next sentence. We are not saying that it was definitely due to your lack of partnership. No one could possibly know that. I would assume, based on our biblical examples, that God does give promises. We are just wondering if he *also* gives invitations. We are just wondering together about how far reaching our part in the story might be. We're exploring the "what if."

Just last night my client told me what God has shown her. She saw her estranged husband with a black skeleton. Then it fell from him like scales and the Lord built new bones within him; white and bright. She took this as a promise, a promise that her husband will be healed of his narcissism and cruelty and that their marriage will be restored. "What do you think your role is in that happening?" I asked. "Just to believe it I guess." "What if there's more you can offer?" I suggested. We explored this partnership idea together.

We came together in prayer and brought her husband before the Lord. We saw him in our mind's eye and offered our imagination to God for his use, like bandwidth. As we prayed for him, we spoke against that black skeleton and called it to fall. We praised God for his desire to bring clean, white bones to this man and we called them forward. We asked/imagined God pouring loving conviction and clarity into his heart. We asked/imagined him surrendering and all of his rebellion melting away. We asked/imagined God wrapping his love around her husband and meeting him in his most wounded places. We asked/imagined God speaking to his wounds and bringing them to peace. We saw the new white bones beginning to form and called them to be in Jesus' name. We both felt hope and joy rising up within us on behalf of her husband. We praised God and thanked him for whatever he had just done with our offering of partnership with him. "That is your homework," I explained. "Pour into this vision with God. With your prayers, say, "Yes Lord! I see your vision! Let's do it!"

When the Lord gives you an impression, a word or a vision of something wonderful, ask about your contribution. Maybe it is a promise and your only part is to rejoice. But maybe it is an invitation awaiting your partnership. How magnificent would it be to collaborate with him in a grand possibility?

An Honest Thank You

O.k., it's time for number three; the third thing I can always do that makes a difference even when faith is weak:

3. I can honestly thank him
for whatever my offering accomplished.

Do you remember in Chapter 8 when we talked about manipulative gratefulness? Aggressive theological underdog "thanks" God as a means of forcing his hand, as if the "thank you" obligates him to do the thing you've asked. But true gratefulness is honest. It thanks for what really is, not for what we're demanding. If the first two are true, that all intention lands, and imagination lands particularly heavily, then I have something to be honestly grateful for. When I offer my drop in that bucket, my imagination as bandwidth before the Lord, I can be confident that it did something, even if incremental. Therefore, I'm thankful. I can thank God without manipulation or falsehood. I don't have to pretend that the pinky is whole. I can be confident that *something* occurred; that if my prayer was in line with his desires he matched my donation. "Thank you God for whatever you just did with my offering."

And then even more happens.

You see, honest gratefulness weighs even more than imagination. True thanksgiving is like subatomic iron. It is more constitutive than hope, more creative than desire. Gratefulness changes things. That's one of the reasons he calls us to "give thanks in all circumstances."

He's known all along that our thanksgiving brings about life. He "inhabits our praise!"[130] It may be new to us, but he could see the particles all along.

Creative Prayer

"Faith is creative," stated Smith Wigglesworth simply. We've been referring to Elijah and his prayer to stop the rain in 1 Kings. Do you remember how it looked when he prayed for the rain's return? He went to the top of Mount Carmel to pray. The Lord had already told him that it was time for the rain to return so he knew where to pour in his contribution. He had fostered intimacy, he had listened, so he knew what the Lord was up to. He knew where to jump in and help.

Then he offered himself, he moved. He bent down with "his face between his knees" and prayed. But nothing happened. At this point, Elijah the UpperDog did not sigh and say, "Well, it must not really be the Lord's will." He did not say, "Man! I'm such a failure! Nothing happened!" He simply offered again, moved again. He knew that his prayers were accumulating, being matched by the Father. Each time he poured a drop into that bucket, he sent his servant out to check the horizon. Clearly he honestly expected something to happen. This went on for a full seven rounds before the servant finally returned with the good news. "There is a small cloud, the size of a man's hand, rising out of the sea," he reported. Elijah literally got up that minute and told Ahab he'd better saddle up the horses and get going before the rain stops him.

This is the account that James is referring to when he utters one of our favorite quotes: "The prayer of a righteous man is powerful and effective."[131] The very next verse is, "Elijah was a man just like us. He prayed that it would not rain and it did not rain on the land for three and a half years. Again he prayed and the heavens gave rain and the earth produced its crops" (paraphrased).

Unapologetically, James, inspired by the Holy Spirit of the Living God, assumes that you will do the same. He assumes that your exploits in prayer will be as measurable. He is using this account of Elijah as an example not an exception. You might say, "Well that's great but I'm not Elijah." And James would say, "Wanna bet?"

When you cultivate your relationship with God, when you abide in him, pour your heart out without reservation. Lay your guts on the table before him like a split fish. Hold nothing back. When you ask for direction, pay attention and expect to get it. Move on suspected promptings. And when you come to partnering prayer, when it's time to stop the rain, consider these three things.

1. Have you listened? Are you aligned with what the Lord is up to?
2. Secondly, ask yourself about your expectation. Do you really expect, really know that your prayer is causing something to happen in unseen realms? If not, repent and ask for him to grow your faith. Then proceed, employing big imagination where faith is small.
3. Honestly thank him for what he's just done with your offering, visible or not.

Partnering In General Will

One of our practitioners tells this story. She was driving through her small town one day when she noticed a new sign on one of the buildings. An adult bookstore had opened in her neighborhood. This was upsetting and sad for her. She loved her town and knew the moral decay this new business would generate. She also knew the Lord. She knew that it is his general will that we live in sexual purity. Based on his character alone, she knew he would not be in favor of the development. She decided to pray. Every day, as she drove past that shop, she prayed for the closure of the business and for conviction and salvation for the owners and patrons. She pushed back the enemy's hold. She prayed for a restoration of sexual morality in her town. She dropped her offerings into that bucket each day, one by one. Each time she thanked God for whatever he was doing with her prayers. Within two months, the bookstore closed. Now they have a yogurt shop.

We can always pour into God's general will. God is longing to eradicate evils all around us all the time, and our participation is required. He decided to make US the hands and feet instead of just using his own. Could he have closed down that shop without her prayer partnership? Of course he could. But he has chosen not to run the show alone.

Healing is another example. We know two things about God that again fall into that dynamic tension category. Generally he wants our wholeness. He's a fan of healing. You cannot read the account of Jesus' time here and come away with any other conclusion. And at the same time, he has appointed it that every man should die and contrary to the aggressor's belief, we do not always know when that is. Just because our hearts feel like everyone should live to a ripe old age doesn't mean it's the design of the Father. His general desire for our wholeness doesn't mean he can't be using an illness or deformity for his purposes. It is his prerogative to do so.

Agnes Sanford talked about having to learn this lesson. She learned to hear "no" as well as "yes." Because of the powerful gifting she experienced, she was often inundated with prayer requests. She learned to ask God if he had healing for that person and if he wanted to use her. Sometimes she would hear that he did not have healing, that it was this person's time to die. In those circumstances, she offered comfort. Remember, his will is dynamic.

Therefore, whenever we come to healing prayer where we haven't been given specific directions, we must come combining faith with submission. We must be willing to offer all we have: our honest expectation and trust that our prayers carry weight, our rich imagination, and our gratefulness, all while maintaining a submissive heart—a heart that says, "Here's all I have to offer and I know it counts. I won't hold back, even though I can't control the outcome. Your will be done."

Partnering in Specifics

But then there are those Elijah times. I'm confident that there have been many of them in my own lifetime and in yours that we didn't recognize. Again, Elijah was not an exception but an example. If you don't think so, take it up with James. There are moments when God says, "Work with me here. Let's get something done."

We were gathered together in the little rustic meeting room at the mountain ranch where we were about to open our annual Master's Retreat for Splankna. We sat in our little circle, like we always do, with the snow falling softly outside and we prayed over the weekend. We laid ourselves out before the Lord and invited him to use us, to lead our minds and hearts all weekend. I gave him the teaching content and invited him to revamp it anywhere he would like. We gathered up any enemy rights or presence there and removed it, set it into the courts in the heavens. We took apart any of the enemy's rights as long as we were renting the facility and dedicated everything to the Kingdom. And then several of us had the same sudden thought.

It came spontaneously to mind that God was inviting us as well. He was prompting us to remove the enemy's right and influence over that facility permanently, not just for our weekend. Now usually, because of the authority structure in the universe, it would not be within our spiritual right to clean this land permanently because it is not ours. We just have a measure of authority while we're renting it, much like when we're in a hotel room for the weekend. But God seemed to be saying that we had a special provision; that we were being granted the grace and authority to act as owners would. Someone spoke up with that thought and it was confirmed by others. We thanked God and excitedly changed our posture. We started partnering prayer over the ranch.

We asked God to bring to mind anything he would have us repent of on behalf of the land and the group that runs the ministry there. We attended to what came to mind, seeing everything as we prayed it. After a little while, when that seemed complete, we revoked the enemy's right and influence over the land and the ministry once and for all. We gave it freshly to the Lord and rededicated it to his purposes. We asked him to pour down his blessing, imagining and thanking him all the while. God wanted to give that land and its ministry a clean sweep, a do-over, and he asked us to saddle up.

Partner Splankna Style

If God is your partner, make your plans BIG!
~ D.L. Moody

The reason we're so invested in exploring more active partnership with God is because we do Splankna Therapy and it affords an unusually literal way to partner. Its design *requires* partnership with God. Our years of experiencing such close collaboration with God through Splankna have been challenging and rich. Because of our familiarity with this kind of partnership with God through Splankna, we are particularly passionate about calling the Body of Christ to more intimacy and more palpable cooperation with our Father. We'll use it here as an example. But please know it is just one of a million styles open to you.

What is Splankna Therapy?

Splankna Therapy is a mind-body procedure for alleviating emotional trauma. It incorporates several different tools from a sub-field within psychology called "energy psychology." Energy psychology is the collection of tools that use the same system in the body that acupuncture and chiropractic are based on, for the purpose of releasing emotional trauma that is physiologically stored. The problem with the field is that it has been developed from an almost exclusively new age worldview. Splankna's call has been to redeem the tools themselves, remove the new age theology and ground these effective mind-body mechanisms back into a biblical foundation where they belong. Only God should get the credit for how his creation works.

The basic theory of energy psychology is that every emotion we ever feel, every thought, memory, decision, etc. throughout our lives is stored in the body like a hard drive. Remember how we've established that at the subatomic level of creation thoughts and emotions have weight, frequency? Well our bodies catalogue every one of these frequencies. We are all walking conglomerations of every experience we've ever had. If we could crack open the subconscious database and look inside, we would be able to trace current emotional symptoms back to their origins. We would be able to trace back today's anxiety to grade school bullying, or today's depression to a first miscarriage.

When a new client comes in (let's call him Adam), he usually has a presenting problem. It could be anything one would take to traditional psychological counseling. Maybe he's struggling with anger or depression, anxiety or addiction. Whatever the issue, he'll describe the problem, its history and his best guess at its root cause. The Splankna practitioner will gather the usual notes and then explain how the protocol works, and they will begin with prayer.

A Splankna Session Begins With Prayer

"Lord God, will you please call to our spirits that are seated in Jesus and raise up that place in us into strong leadership? As much as we know how to, we both hand ourselves over to you now completely. We lay ourselves at your feet as living sacrifices. Please gather us where we're broken and bring everything under the authority of your Spirit. In your Name Lord Jesus we take authority over the soul. We close down all the

chaos and enemy activity there and we ask you, Lord Jesus, to lay your hand now on the soul. Set it to perfect peace and surrender."

"Lord Jesus we trust you to handle the warfare. Will you please collect all warfare that has any right to us, to both of us, and lock it under your feet. If we need any backup will you send that for us please? Arrange the heavens around us in peace and strength. Please go before us in battle.

"Lord we need you to handle our will. Please move through us now in your Spirit and everywhere our will is stubborn for any reason. Melt our will down now by your power. Align our will with your own so that we can surrender to you. Share your desire with us so that we can want what you're wanting for this session."

"Lord God, may I (practitioner) please have your blessing to be completely effective in your hand today and for your perfect objectivity as we work. Will you please open my ears to hear your lead? May I please have your anointing to move Adam past me wherever that applies? Holy Spirit, please stir your presence in us. Please rest on us in leadership and authority. Cause us to be able to partner with you far past our own strength."

"Lord God, we know that you know Adam's heart better than we do. You know everything he's ever experienced and you know your plans for him. We trust your leadership for this session. Will you please come now and seek out the place in his heart that you choose to work on today? Holy Spirit, mark out the steps you would have us take and we will follow you. Will you reveal to his heart the joy in what you are offering him? Will you please speak to his heart just what he needs to hear in order to follow you there?"

"May your whole will be done. May your Kingdom be advanced in everything we say and do. In your name Lord Jesus, Amen"

They Muscle Test to Begin the Work

Splankna Therapy uses muscle testing as a diagnostic tool. Muscle testing is based on the theory that any major muscle will respond to energetic shifts that go off in the body. All thoughts have a frequency on the subatomic level. So when the practitioner asks Adam a question, the frequency of her meaning passes between them and it hits Adam's body as a "match" or "mismatch." When Adam's body responds with congruence to an idea, it shifts his energy system and that shift shows up in his muscle. It is a way to check into that subconscious database.

For instance, if the practitioner asked whether the root emotion around a particular trauma is "anger," if Adam's subconscious database is congruent with that idea (frequency), his muscle will respond as well (weak vs. strong). Because the body naturally responds to ideas this way, a muscle test can be used as a crude little yes/no tool. Muscle testing is not a perfect tool, but still a useful one as long as it is covered by prayer. There are several things that can cause a muscle to react and truth is just one of them, so you always have to take a muscle test with a heavy grain of salt.

Muscle testing is where the partnership really finds its nuts and bolts in Splankna Therapy. As you read in the example opening prayer, the practitioner and client are both inviting the Spirit of God to come and work in the client's heart. They have invited God to choose the work HE would like to do. They offer the tool to God for his use and invite the Spirit to search through Adam's subconscious database and choose the content he wants to address. When you come before the Lord and invite him to do anything he'd like to do in your heart...

He does.

The Spirit of God actually does come and search through Adam's system. Why wouldn't he? God survey's all that Adam carries—every moment he's known, every emotion he's felt, every though and agreement, vow and lie and the Spirit marks the content to be addressed. Adam's and his practitioner trust in simple faith that the Spirit of God did just choose a chunk of emotional trauma to work with in him. The muscle test is simply the tool they use to ask Adam's own heart/subconscious, "Okay, where in your database did the Spirit just choose?" Since Adam's own heart and body have awareness of the content the Spirit just chose, the muscle will respond.

First they ascertain what specific age they're addressing in Adam's history. Then they test for the "central emotion." The central emotion is the one the client felt in the moment of the trauma that best represents the theme of the event. For instance, if the trauma was a father leaving, the central emotion might be "Grief" or "Abandonment." They work through a simple Emotion Chart to help identify which emotions the client felt and stored in body memory and the subconscious hard drive in this particular moment of trauma.

They Clear Each of the Traumatic Emotions

The proper combination of touch and thought allows the body to release each trauma emotion like letting go of an electrical charge. The client touches the acupuncture point on his own body while thinking about the trauma emotion and how it was felt during the event/age they're addressing. They work through spoken forgiveness statements when needed. They follow these steps to clear all the trauma emotions that were stored from the identified trauma. In our example, the central emotion might be "Grief," then there might be six more trauma emotions that Adam felt/stored when his father left. The Practitioner would walk Adam through clearing all of those emotions one by one and Adam's body would release them on the subatomic level. The closest metaphor is like neutralizing a frequency or an electrical charge. Each emotion would take a few minutes to identify and clear.

They Find the Significant Vow or Lie

Once the emotions are cleared around the identified trauma, it's time to handle the spiritual issue as well. They find the significant vow or lie that the client adopted in the moment of trauma. In prayer together, the client will confess, repent and break agreement with that destructive coping reaction. They ask Jesus to breathe life into all the areas of the client that were affected. If they broke agreement with a lie, they ask Jesus to write the truth where the lie used to be. If they broke a vow, they give that place in the will to Jesus and ask him to seal it to his own will, to establish his permanent reign there.

Results

In the conscious mind, we choose life. We could all wake up any morning and decide to break agreement with lies we see operating in our lives. But when we attempt that, it isn't always as fruitful as we hope. This is partly because as Romans 7 explains, there is a conflict in our will. The "spirit man" chooses life but our brokenness chooses death. Splankna therapy walks the client through these steps of clearing traumatic emotions because when the painful emotions around a trauma are released, the whole being is freed up to "agree" with finally breaking that lie or vow and change can occur. The client will notice that when something happens in life that would normally "trigger" the symptom, they're peaceful instead of reactive.

And we praise God.

How's that for partnership! It has been a fascinating and wonderful adventure to work with God this way and see him move in such tangible, measurable ways in our clients' lives. The secondary blessings have also been amazing—the functional development of faith and intimacy.

One of the criticisms we commonly hear is, "Doesn't this just take people away from trusting in God for healing?" People hear about steps and tools and think it's a *substitute* for pursuing God— an alternative. But that couldn't be further from the truth. Our experience, and the experience of the hundreds of practitioners we have trained, is that this little mechanism offers a unique, substantial, intimate way to co-operate with the Father. Beautiful partnership. Beautiful fruit. And both intimacy and hearing grow and grow through its use. Practitioners and clients alike consistently report growing closer to God through this process, not farther. If it were any other way, we would've ceased development years ago. Not only this way, but any way you can find to place yourself in literal dependence upon God's involvement will serve hearing and intimacy, not diminish it.

Let's Go With That

One of the terrific nuances of mind-body work is that if you do it "wrong," it just misses rather than causing harm. For instance, if the accurate emotion a client needed to clear was "insecurity" and the practitioner miss-tested and cleared "resentment," the client's body would just receive the input as "unrecognized." It simply misses rather than doing harm. This is a great metaphor to partnership on every level.

I say it to every group of new practitioners in training. I tell them while they're in practice dyads that as I walk around the room supervising I want to hear a lot of "Let's go with that." What I mean is that since they can't cause harm, I want them to take a risk. If they think they might be reading a muscle test a particular way, "go with it." If it's wrong it will only miss. We've learned over time that the best way to learn the subtle sensitivity of muscle testing is to push against your natural tendency to double and triple check things and just "go with it."

All partnership requires this kind of risk. God is a big fan of it. The same way that new Splankna trainees have the freedom to risk, we all have freedom to risk with God. If you pursue him for direction and you think he might be giving an inclination, "go with it." That's the only way to test it. The only way to find out if it was his prompting or not is to go with it, move on it, and allow him the opportunity to respond to your risk. He will respond. He will close a door when you get off track and he will confirm and open the next door when you're aligned. Splankna has taught us how literally we can trust his responses to our unsure offerings.

Considering the fact that we rarely get divine sticky notes from the clouds, we have to learn to take chances. We either have to live in theological isolation, never giving our choices to God more than general morality, or we have to move and trust he'll re-direct us. As a teenager I realized I could never really *know* God's specific will in a particular situation. Not with that writing on the wall certainty. I realized that the only options are risk or practical atheism. I chose this strategy then and it's a keeper. "Let's go with that." God is trustworthy to handle your reckless attempt at obedience. Sometimes it's "let's give to that charity." Sometimes it's "let's move to China." But it's always a ride. Splankna Therapy has been our adventure in partnership. God meets us here. He's ready to meet you somewhere too.

We have witnessed God lifting debilitating depression and anxiety in a single sitting, toddlers relieved of trichotillomania (the compulsive pulling out of one's hair), marriages restored and rage permanently lifted. We've watched him attend to hurts so personally and thoroughly that it brings us to tears. He has healed all manner of physical symptoms that were emotionally rooted. He has brought fierce conviction and overcoming hope. Truly there isn't a word strong enough to describe the honor and privilege it has been to partner with him in these things.

We considered including stories at this point of some of the specific miracles God has performed through our tool, but this book isn't about Splankna. It's about being UpperDogs, both in Ambassadorship and in Partnership and Splankna is just one of innumerable ways to participate. It's one example of a million and one. God is dying to partner with you. He designed you with a personal way to move with him. It's in your blood. He's on the edge of his seat, waiting for you to engage

Engage

"Come on, get in there. Engage! Take the shot kid, take the shot!.
You can engage any time, Maverick."
- Top Gun

Whether culturally or with God, decide something today. Decide to move. Decide to engage. Decide that you *really* believe what the Scriptures say about who you are and what this story is about. Take seriously your position as a representative and as a collaborator. Decide to live like an UpperDog. The days are short.

The Line

We laid down on our backs and relaxed. The ballroom was dark and everything was quiet. We were in for a guided imagery session. "Pathways" was a Christian personal growth seminar in the 90's that my cousins had encouraged me to attend. So there I was, ready to grow. "Close your eyes and allow your imagination to follow this story. Imagine that you're standing in a long line" the speaker began. "There are twenty or so people in front of you and the line ends at an imposing white door. When your turn comes, you will walk through that door and meet God. You will experience final judgment. This is your time to meet the Lord and give an account of your life here on earth. But for now, you are just waiting."

The speaker continued, "Notice the people in front of you and behind you. How do they look? Are they nervous? Are they arrogant?" I imagined people wringing their hands, their eyes darting around, their foreheads sweating. "Notice your own emotions" the speaker said. "What do you feel? What are the things you'll have to confess before God? What are the choices you regret, the words you wish you'd never spoken? The door opens and the next person in line walks through. It closes behind them. What do you think they're experiencing?"

My mind moved back and forth, surveying my life as if from an eagle-eye view. My memories swirled around me like currents in water. "What is the sum of my life? How will it look to God?" The line moved forward again. As my mind relaxed into the exercise, the imagery was clearer. A woman near the front fell to her knees in tears. A man behind me was cursing under his breath. Time passed as we all took account of every careless word, every cup of water never given. "Now you're next in line," the speaker continued. "Your turn is about to come. What will you say to the Holy One? Place your hand on the doorknob. Are you ready?" I noticed that I was holding my breath. "They've called your name. Turn the knob and open the door."

I could feel the cool iron in the palm of my hand. The door was heavy but silent as it opened. The moment I took a step inside I hit the floor, face to the ground in response to his glory and majesty. I had nothing to say. Without looking, I knew he was sitting before me on his throne, splendid and beaming, but my only first response was to bow before him. And then the surprising thing happened. My mind, lost in the moment, took a turn I wouldn't have expected. From my position there on the ground, I suddenly looked up, looked him in the eyes and smiled. He smiled back. My heart exploded with the depth of our private friendship and I sprinted into his arms.

That day is really going to come. How will it feel to you?

The Room

A colleague of mine told me about a tool she uses to connect with God. She is single and has a particularly deep longing for intimacy with him. She asked him to create a special space, a room that was just theirs where they could meet and talk. She wanted to have a place to imagine that she was meeting with him in prayer. As she prayed about that and journaled, God brought a specific room to her mind's eye. It was a bedroom, decked out in rich purple. She knew that he was inviting her as his bride to their private place where no one else could go. Meeting him there has served her intimacy with him over the years.

I was intrigued by the idea so I brought it to God myself. "Could I have a special room with you too?' I asked. "I would love that." As I prayed and journaled he seemed to meet my request, but in a different way than my friend had experienced. In my mind's eye, as I opened the door to "our room" it was not a bedroom at all. It was like a dark cave, cool and damp. "Really God? A cave? What are you trying to say to me here?" But then I noticed something as my eyes adjusted. The walls and ceilings were bejeweled. They were covered in imbedded, sparkling gem stones, colorful and spectacular. It reminded me of the diamond mine of the seven dwarfs! "Wow! It's beautiful!" I said. "These jewels are yours," he said. They are all the people you've impacted, all the hearts you've healed with me." I was overcome as the tears ran down my cheeks.

The privilege of partnering with him is unparalleled and the result is eternal. Everything you do with God is permanent. It never goes to waste and it adorns the "bride." Do you remember being moved by Ray Boltz' song, "Thank You For Giving To The Lord?" It chokes you up whether you like it or not, doesn't it? There's a good reason for that. Your spirit knows that the day is really coming. The skin on your knee is going to hit actual gravel and you will see him face to face. Your righteousness is handled. Jesus paid for it and the debt is cancelled. But what about your contribution? We will all give an account on that day and not only for righteousness. We will give an account for contribution as well. "The powerful play goes on and you may contribute a verse."[132] You may contribute a verse. Don't forfeit your chance. It will matter on that day.

The Talents

Several times we've mentioned the parable of the talents in Matthew 25 and Luke 19. We've all heard sermons on it, I'm sure. Three guys are given "talents" by their master to reign over while he's gone. These "talents" represent all of the potential we're given: resources, skills, opportunities, gifting, everything. The master is saying, "Here, I'm giving you a portion to manage. Do your best with it." When he returns he finds that two of them have been busy. They have done something productive with what was entrusted to them. They have multiplied the master's account, added to his estate. But one of them responded differently. Scripture gives us a peek into his thought process: "My master is a hard man," he thinks to himself. "He reaps where he does not sow." "I'd better keep safe what he entrusted to me. I'd better not risk anything and mess it up." So he does the famous thing. He buries his talent and keeps it safe. When the master returns he thinks he's done well. He presents his "safe," undeveloped investment before the master and awaits his praise. But you know how the story ends. It does not go well for this guy. The master doesn't just disapprove, he calls him "wicked" and casts him away. Now I've heard this story a million times (it feels like). I remember as a little girl thinking, "Wow God, aren't you being a little harsh with the guy? I mean, he's just scared. Give a guy a break!"

We shrink back from ambassadorship and avoid the risk of partnership because we're afraid. That's what it really comes down to. And we give each other lots of grace over that, don't we? "Oh, I understand. I know it's hard. I don't do any better myself. Good thing there's grace over us, right?" But I wonder if our Master is so casual about it. There's a quiet little secret in Scripture that no one ever talks about. There are several places in addition to this one that imply an interesting thing about heaven: it will not be a uniform experience.[133] Salvation itself relies on Jesus alone. We're clear on that. His sacrifice paid for our sin and our trust in his atonement is what enables us to live in heaven in intimacy with a Holy God. There is no contribution that can buy your salvation. But we do have another dynamic tension here: grace vs. works.

The body of Christ has worked hard on grace in the last several decades. We've knocked ourselves out to get clear on the fact that Jesus' atonement paid for it all. You see, the theological imbalance of yore said, "You'd better save your neighbors or you're going to hell!" We rallied against that self-sufficient, "works-oriented" religion. But in our attempt to avoid that imbalance, we've created another one. In our zeal to reject self-sufficiency we have taken our contributions out of the equation all together. We see contribution only in terms of "proof" of salvation, like your works are just a superfluous outgrowth of your saved state. You do good works "as a thank you" to God for saving you. Yes, this is true. We do contribute out of gratefulness and love. But that theology makes it sound like it doesn't matter what we do or do not contribute. Our contribution is just extra, an aside, a sign of salvation.

I contend that there is even more going on here. What if our contributions in this life bear directly on the next? Our contributions don't save us, but what if they affect the next chapter? What if my experience of heaven, my role there and my (dare I say) "status" there are all impacted by what I do *here* with my "talent"? The saved are not meant to simply enjoy their salvation. They are not mere benefactors of the Gospel. They are meant to be partners in the creation of a Kingdom! A Kingdom with no end.

Your opportunities are everywhere. Literally every moment of your life is ripe with potential, with possibility to affect a social moment, to speak a powerful truth, to drop some color into the mix. Did you ever read Frank Peretti's, *This Present Darkness*?[134] One of the scenes he describes has always stayed in my mind. The main character in the novel is distraught and goes into the church building. He's there alone, agonizing, worrying. Peretti then describes the unseen realm all around the man. The building is full of taunting, torturous demons, throwing threats and accusation toward the character one after another. It is a gruesome image. There are angels present as well. They surround the upper area of the ceiling, hands poised on their swords. "*Pray…*" they whisper intently. "Come on, PRAY!" They are bound unless he will. When he finally utters the first word of a prayer, they tear out their swords and vanquish his enemies.

In this moment, your God is poised and ready, his hand on his sword.

"*Engage…*" he implores.

"Come on, ENGAGE!"

Afterward

Partnership In Writing This Book

Sarah's Perspective

Late one evening I sent my father a copy of Chapter 6 of this book. I had just finished it and I was excited. I wanted to share it. He read it and called me to talk about it. "How did you write that so quickly?" he asked. "Well actually, Dad, I wrote it just like the book itself describes." I then gave him the play-by-play of my afternoon of writing. After my description, he said, "You've got to share that with the reader. Your process of writing this book is a perfect example of its content." And it's true. Our experience of writing this (and my experience of writing the *Splankna* book as well) is another example of partnership in action.

Because so many years had already gone into the development of Splankna Therapy and the content that our training institute provides, I knew when the first book was finished that this one was already in preparation. As I said in the introduction chapter, this book is the "theology discussion" we have at the outset of our Level 2, Advanced Training. So when the time came to get to work, and Heather and I had decided to make this book a joint venture, we began the obvious way. We got together and brought it before God. "Okay Lord, here we are. We think you're calling us to write this *UpperDogs* book, so we lay the whole idea out before you as a sacrifice." We committed ourselves and the project to him and his purposes. We asked him to wrap his hands around our minds and direct us in his own thoughts. We invited the Holy Spirit to rise in us and asked him to build that special connection with us that the disciples had, that inspiration connection. We asked that the right people would read it, that it would be "alive" like his Word is. We thanked him for the honor of it all.

We began the work with a global outline of ideas, working around different options, different organization of thought, waiting and listening. We have brought enough idea-tasks before him by now to know how he deals with us. We know that if we bring him our thoughts and let him work in them, they will eventually congeal. The moment will come when things "click" and we both agree and resonate with it. That process took an evening in regards to the book's outline and then we assigned sections for each of us to start writing. At the close of the night we invited God to continue to rearrange anything we had come up with. We're always wanting to hold an inviting position towards him—a cooperative, expectant posture.

Then came the nitty gritty.

Every time either one of us sat down to write, without fail, we would quiet ourselves before the Lord. Attempting to write a useful book on theology is a serious undertaking. It is not to be taken lightly. We're both aware that we cannot afford to be casual with it. We cannot glibly assume we've "got this." We're thoroughly dependent on his partnership, on his wisdom moving through us. In our own power alone, the end product would be pitiful. After all, who has known his thoughts? Who has instructed him? Why would we think we should speak with authority about the things of God? Only he knows what is true. Only he knows his plans for this book, what he wants to do with it, who he wants to impact and how. So every time we lay ourselves out before him, we invite him to move in us in that same way we did in the beginning. We address any emotional content that might be in the way, like self-consciousness, confusion or pride. We pray everything that comes to mind both on the "down side" (i.e. any warfare elements) and on the "up side" (i.e. any blessing or anointing, inspiration, etc.) And then we move and trust.

We start to put down words, listening, paying attention to ideas, illustrations, memories that might come to mind. If we write a section that feels "off," we bring it before him and invite his re-write. We also involved godly counsel. We shared the book's content, at different stages, with several fellow believers and asked for their feedback and critique. Before we read through any of those critiques, we would ask God to place one of those filters over the content so that we could completely receive what he had for us there and nothing else.

Collaboration with God is natural if you assume he's involved. Our assumption of his nearness makes questioning, inviting and trusting easier. It also makes it easier to trust the outcome of partnership. It avails our hearts of the joy *he* feels in this book. We hope you've felt some of that too.

Heather's Perspective

Every time I sat down with God to write this book, it was a unique experience. I certainly learned more about my strengths and weaknesses. I learned how vitally important it is to partner with God. I would suggest seeking God's guidance continually when he gives you a job. God revealed to me the importance of beginning with prayer. There were days when the Holy Spirit took over and I flew through the writing process. I'd look at the clock and realize that several hours had flown by and I had just written several pages. I loved those days. I would look back over what I wrote with amazement and think, "Did I really just write that?" Other times, when I wasn't centered with God, I would struggle to write a sentence.

Through the leading of the Holy Spirit, we learned things about ourselves. We learned more about our Father's heart. We cried, we laughed, we praised and there were times we were even shaken by the profound revelations that he gave us. There were moments of paralysis, when we were overwhelmed by Him and were unable to move. Those times we would press into him even more for resources. He would pull us out and put our feet back on solid ground. We had feelings of inadequacy mixed with profound gratitude to be his voice in this area. There were even times when we would call each other and say, "I'm sorry I can't write today. I'm too busy *being* an UpperDog to write about it!" Which again, just brought us back to profound gratitude.

Most importantly, every time we sat down to write we began with prayer. Our prayer style is very similar to the opening prayer in a Splankna session. We start with praising God for allowing us to walk in this adventure with him. Seriously, does it get any better than that? Marveling in the countless ways that he had previously led, we began with completely saturating ourselves in thankfulness and awe of God.

After praising him, we asked God to take all of our heavy burdens, brokenness and anything else that would hinder us from doing his work. We asked him to hold all that we carry in his hands and empower us by the Holy Spirit to do his will in writing this book. We specifically asked him to break our wills and line them up with his own. We want all that he wants for this book—nothing more, nothing less.

Next we would clean house by gathering up all of the warfare and plans of the enemy against us individually and against the book. We would imagine that all of the warfare was locked away in his heavenly courts unable to operate or affect us in any way. We asked Jesus to stand between us and the enemy as we wrote and that he would assign extra backup in the form of warrior angels. We asked God to replace all of the enemy's influence in our lives with the Holy Spirit, asking him to anoint us by his Spirit… for power, love and wisdom.

After we prayed all of this we would ask and listen, to see if God had anything else for us to pray. Do we need to pray something else on the blessing side, the warfare side? Whatever he brought to mind we prayed.

When we felt a sense of completion in this "set-up" prayer, we asked God to bring to mind any negative emotions we needed to let go of. If he brought an emotion to mind we would apply the Splankna protocol to clear those emotions. Then we asked if we needed to download any positive emotions; we call them creative emotions in our protocol. We would then use our imaginations to partner with him to envision whatever he wanted us to see. Sometimes there was a need to focus on being completely surrendered. Sometimes we needed to let the excitement of the Holy Spirit fill us.

One particular morning, I woke up with an idea that I was sure was from the Holy Spirit. As I went about my morning, getting kids off to school and such, the idea began to fade away. After I prayed and applied the Splankna tools, I instantly remembered what God had told me in the morning. That was one of my best writing days. He is trustworthy to lead our thoughts when we invite him.

Some days I was so impressed with the Holy Spirit's leading that I couldn't wait to share that day's writing with someone. I would read it to my children (ages 8-15) as soon as they got home from school. They started asking me to read more excerpts. In fact my 12 year old, Ethan, asked if he could edit the book when we were finished. (How cute is that?)

Thank you God! Thank you for entrusting this task into our hands. Thank you for teaching us so much. Thank you for the profound privilege of waking up every day and you are there. You look on us in love and hold your hand out to us. You invite us to be a part of something bigger than ourselves. I look forward to our daily adventures, no matter if the adventure is ministering to my family by preparing a special recipe, meeting with a friend to represent your love, or writing a book. Everything we do together is so much better than when I try to do it myself. Thank you most of all for teaching me this lesson.

About The Authors

Heather & Sarah getting their caricatures drawn in Times Square after a Splankna Training.

Sarah Thiessen is a private practitioner, speaker and the founder of the Splankna Therapy Institute in Denver, Colorado. She is a licensed Marriage & Family Therapist and a Licensed Professional Counselor. She holds undergraduate and graduate degrees from Abilene Christian University and is the author of the innovative book, *Splankna*. She lives in Colorado with her husband Jon and three children.

Heather Hughes is a private practitioner, speaker and Certified Life Coach. She is a developer and assistant director of the Splankna Therapy Institute. She lives in Colorado with her husband Joe and four children.

Endnotes

1   W. Watts Biggers, *Underdog*, (NBC, 1964.)

2   David Wilcox, *Glory*, Turning Point, 1997.

3   Matthew 28:16-20

4   John 12:32

5   1 John 4:8

6   John 8:11

7   1 Corinthians 6:7

8   Steve Bond, *A Transformed Life Preserves the Unity*; SermonCentral.com,

9   Matthew 24:42

10   Brennan Manning, *The Ragamuffin Gospel* (Multnomah Books, 2005).

11   Matthew 25:21

12   Proverbs 16:18

13   Matthew 5:21

14   Matthew 20:21

15   2 Chronicles 7:14

16   G. K. Chesterton, *Tremendous Trifles*, (HardPress Publishing, 2010).

17   C. S. Lewis, *The Problem Of Pain*, (MacMillan & Co, 1974).

18   I Thessalonians 5:18

19   Numbers 21:9

20   2 Kings 5:14

21   John 9:6

22   Numbers 17

23   Exodus 7:10

24   Jeremiah 19:10

25   2 Corinthians 6:16

26   Genesis 1:26

[27] Colossians 1:16

[28] Sarah Thiessen, *Splankna: The Redemption of Energy Healing for the Kingdom of God*, (Crosshouse Publishing, 2011).

[29] Psalm 24:1

[30] Tom Doyle, *Breakthrough: The Return Of Hope To The Middle East* (Biblica Publishing, 2008) pp. 51-52.

[31] Dr. Emerson Eggerichs, *Love and Respect* (Thomas Nelson, 2004).

[32] www.compassion.com

[33] www.wvi.org

[34] www.samaritanspurse.org

[35] Rich Deem, *Famous Scientists Who Believed In God,* godsandscience.org.

[36] Francis Bacon, *Essays, Civil and Moral*, The Harvard Classics. 1909–14.

[37] Ronald Clark, *Einstein: The Life and Times*, London, Hodder and Stoughton Ltd., 1973, 33

[38] Werner Gitt, *In The Beginning Was Information* (Master Books, 2006). William A. Dembski, *Intelligent Design: The Bridge Between Science and Theology* (IVP Academic, 2002).

[39] Isaiah 22:13

[40] Stacy Trasancos, *Science Was Born Of Christianity – The Teaching of Fr. Stanley L. Jaki,* (Habitation of Chinham Publishing, 2014).

[41] I Corinthians 2:16

[42] Neil T. Anderson, *Victory Over The Darkness*, (Bethany House Publishers, 2000).

[43] John 10:10

[44] I Corinthians 2:13

[45] Exodus 13:9

[46] 2 Thessalonians 3:10-12

[47] Psalm 50:10

[48] Luke 12:27, Matthew 10:30, Proverbs 10:3

[49] Victor Hugo, *Les Miserables,* (A. Lacroix, Verboeckhoven & Cie., 1862).

[50] IBID.

[51] 1 Thessalonians 4:13

52   American Association of Suicidology, 2014.

53   Hebrews 12:2

54   Daniel 10:13

55   John 15:20

56   Tom Doyle, *Breakthrough: The Return Of Hope To The Middle East* (Biblica Publishing, 2008) p. 89.

57   John Foxe, *Foxe's Book of Martyrs,* 15th printing (Flemming H. Revell Co., 1979).

58   Eric Metaxas, *Miracles: What They Are, Why They Happen and How They Can Change Your Life*, (Penguin Random House, 2014).

59   Joel C. Rosenberg, *Epicenter: Why The Current Rumblings In the Middle East Will Change Your Future* (Tyndale, 2006).

60   Doyle, *Breakthrough: The Return Of Hope To The Middle East* (Biblica Publishing, 2008) p. 109.

61   www.cbn.com **(How Christianity is Growing Around the World, By Charles Colson, *Breakpoint Ministry)***

62   www.cbn.com **(How Christianity is Growing Around the World, By Charles Colson, *Breakpoint Ministry)***

63   www.cbn.com **(How Christianity is Growing Around the World, By Charles Colson, *Breakpoint Ministry)***

64   Romans 8:38

65   Matthew 16:18

66   www.Splankna.com/about-us/what-is-splankna/the-witchcraft-question/

67   Ephesians 4:15

68   James 5: 17

69   Francis Chan, *The Forgotten God*, (David C. Cook, 2009).

70   James 1:6

71   Ephesians 1:21

72   Niurka. "Tony Robbins Unleashing the Power," *Success Magazine.* Retrieved October 17, 2011

73   Genesis 3:5

74   Sarah Thiessen, *Splankna: The Redemption of Energy Healing for the Kingdom of God* (CrossHouse, 2011).

[75] Proverbs 16:33

[76] Proverbs 16:1, 9

[77] Romans 8:28

[78] Romans 4:17

[79] Joshua 24:15

[80] Romans 8:29

[81] Matthew 9:29, Mark 10:52

[82] Ephesians 1:21

[83] Ephesians 2:6

[84] Rebecca Brown, *He Came To Set The Captives Free*, (Whitaker House, 1992).

[85] Luke 10:21

[86] Ephesians 1:17-21

[87] Proverbs 3:5

[88] John 16:13

[89] Todd Burpo, *Heaven If For Real*, (Thomas Nelson, 2010).

[90] Matthew 10:16

[91] Mark Virkler, *The Four Keys To Hearing God's Voice*, (CWGMinistries.org, 2010).

[92] Psalm 37:4

[93] Oz Guinness, *The Call: Finding and Fulfilling the Central Purpose of Your Life*, (Thomas Nelson, 2003).
Gary Barkalow, *It's Your Call: What Are You Doing Here?* (David C. Cook, 2010).

[94] 2 Timothy 3:17

[95] Proverbs 22:29

[96] I Corinthians 3:2

[97] John Piper, *Amazing Grace In The Life Of William Wilberforce*, (Crossway, 2007).

[98] Regine Pernoud, *Joan of Arc By Herself and Her Witnesses*, (Scarborough House, 2012, p. 35.)

[99] Hebrews 3:15

[100] John 5:19

[101]   Hebrews 4:12

[102]   Mark Virkler, www.cwgministries.org

[103]   John 16:13

[104]   Amy Grant. "All I Ever Have To Be." Never Alone (Myrrh Records, 1980).

[105]   Steve Shae, *That's Not My Voice*, 2014.

[106]   John Eldredge, *Wild At Heart*, (Thomas Nelson, 2001)

[107]   Luke 7:9

[108]   Romans 8:1

[109]   Ephesians 2:6

[110]   Werner Gitt, *In The Beginning Was Information,* (Master Books, 2006).
William A. Dembski, *Intelligent Design: The Bridge Between Science and Theology*
(IVP Academic, 2002).

[111]   Sarah Thiessen, *Splankna: The Redemption of Energy Healing For The Kingdom* Of God, (CrossHouse Books, 2011).

[112]   Judy Franklin & Ellyn Davis, *The Physics Of Heaven* (Double Portion Publishing, 2012).

[113]   Heisenberg, *Physics and Philosophy,* pp. 58, 81.

[114]   Phil Mason, *Quantum Glory* (XP Publishing, 2012).

[115]   Sarah Thiessen, *Splankna: The Redemption of Energy Healing For The Kingdom* Of God, (CrossHouse Books, 2011).

[116]   Ibid.

[117]   Ibid.

[118]   Luke 5:17

[119]   Malachi 3:10

[120]   2 Chronicles 7:14

[121]   Agnes Sanford, *The Healing Light,* (Ballantine Books, Revised Edition, 1983).

[122]   Genesis 1:26

[123]   James 1:6

[124]   Acts 3:6

[125]   Caroline Leaf, *Who Switched Off My Brain? Controlling Toxic Thoughts And Emotions* (Thomas Nelson, 2009).

[126] "The Neurobiology of Positive Emotions," Neuroscience and Behavioral Reviews, Vol. 30, Issue 2, 2006, pgs 173-187.

[127] Philippians 4:8

[128] 2 Corinthians 10:5

[129] John Piper, *Desiring God: Confessions of a Christian Hedonist* (Multnomah, 2003).

[130] Psalm 22:3

[131] James 5:17

[132] Peter Weir, Dir., *Dead Poet's Society*, (Touchstone Pictures, 1989).

[133] Daniel 12:3, 2 Corinthians 11:24, Matthew 16:27, 1 Thessalonians 2:19, 1 Corinthians 9:1, Matthew 11:11 and Galatians 4:11

[134] Frank E. Peretti, *This Present Darkness* (Crossways, 1986).

Made in the USA
Monee, IL
30 April 2022

95691499R00163